BRITISH LABOUR STRUGGLES:
CONTEMPORARY PAMPHLETS 1727-1850

TRADE UNIONS

UNDER

THE COMBINATION ACTS

Five Pamphlets

1799-1823

Arno Press

A New York Times Company/New York 1972

Reprint Edition 1972 by Arno Press Inc.

Reprinted from copies in the Kress Library
Graduate School of Business Administration,
Harvard University

BRITISH LABOUR STRUGGLES: CONTEMPORARY PAMPHLETS 1727-1850
ISBN for complete set: 0-405-04410-0

See last pages for complete listing.

Manufactured in the United States of America

Library of Congress Cataloging in Publication Data
Main entry under title:

Trade unions under the Combination Acts.

    (British labour struggles:
contemporary pamphlets 1727-1850)
    CONTENTS: An abstract of an act, to prevent unlawful
combinations amongst journeymen to raise wages, &c,
[first published 1799].--Rules adopted by the journeymen
millwrights for the well-governing of their society
[first published 1801].--Facts and observations, to prove
the impolicy and dangerous tendency, of the bill now
before Parliament, for limiting the number of apprentices
and other restrictions in the calico printing business
[first published 1807]. [etc.]
    1. Trade-unions--Great Britain. I. Series.
LAW   344'.42'018   72-2550
ISBN 0-405-04441-0

Contents

AN ABSTRACT

OF

AN ACT,

TO PREVENT

UNLAWFUL COMBINATIONS

AMONGST

JOURNEYMEN

TO

RAISE WAGES, &c.

Passed the 19th of July, 1799.

———————

LEEDS:

PRINTED BY EDWARD BAINES.

Abstract of an Act, &c.

I. BE it enacted, That from the passing of this Act, all contracts, covenants, and agreements in writing or not in writing, heretofore entered into by any Journeymen, Manufactures or other Workmen for obtaining any advance of wages, or for lessening or altering their or any of their usual hours or times of working, or for decreasing the quantity of work, or for preventing or hindering any person from employing whom he shall think proper to employ, or for controulling any person carrying on any manufacture, trade, or business, in the management thereof, are hereby declared to be illegal, null, and void, to all intents and purposes whatever.

II. That no Journeymen Workmen or other persons shall, enter into any such agreement, in writing or not in writing, as is hereinbefore declared to be an illegal agreement ; and every Journeyman, Workman, or other person, who, shall be guilty of any of the said offences, being thereof lawfully convicted, upon his own confession, or the oath or oaths of one or more credible witnesses, before any Justice of the Peace for the county, &c where such offence shall be committed, shall, by order of such Justice be confined in the common gaol for any time not exceeding three calendar months, or at the discretion of such Justice shall be committed to some house of correction there to be kept to hard labour for any time not exceeding two calendar months.

III. That every Journeyman or Workman who shall, enter into any combination to obtain an advance of wages, or to lessen or alter the hours of the time of working, or decrease the quantity of work, or who shall, by giving money, or by persuasions or any other means, endeavour to prevent any unemployed Journeyman or Workman, from hiring himself to any manufacturer or tradesman, or shall by any means whatsoever, prevail on any Journeyman or Workman hired in any such manufacture, or business, to leave his work, or who shall hinder, or prevent any manufacturer or tradesman, from employing in his business, such Journeymen, Workmen, and other persons as he think proper, or shall refuse to work with Workman employed to work therein, and who shall be lawfully convicted of any of the said offences, upon his own confession, or on the oath of one or more credible witness or witnesses, before any Justice of the Peace, within three calendar months after the offence shall have been committed, shall, be confined in the common gaol for any time not exceeding three calendar months, or otherwise be committed to some house of correction there to remain and to be kept to hard labour for any time not exceeding two calendar months.

IV. That every person (whether employed

in any such manufacture, trade, or business, or not) who shall attend any meeting for the purpose of entering into any agreement, by this Act declared to be illegal, or of entering into, or continuing any combination for any purpose by this Act declared to be illegal, or give notice to, call upon, persuade, entice, solicit, or intimidate any Workman, or other person employed in any manufacture, or business to attend any such meeting, or who shall collect, any sum of money from any Workmen for any of the purposes aforesaid, or who shall persuade, Workmen, or other persons, to enter into any such combination, or leave their work, or who shall pay any sum of money towards the support of any such illegal combination, and who shall be lawfully convicted within three calendar months after the offence shall have been committed, shall, be confined in the common gaol for any time not exceeding three calendar months, or otherwise be committed to some house of correction, there to be kept to hard labour for any time not exceeding two calendar months.

V. That no person shall at any time after the passing of this Act pay any sum of money, or valuable thing, as a subscription for the purpose of paying any expenses incurred by any person acting contrary to the provisions of this Act, or shall, by payment of money or other means, support workmen, or other persons, for the purpose of inducing them to refuse to work, every person who shall be guilty of such offence, shall forfeit any sum not exceeding ten pounds, and every Journeyman, Workman, and other person, who shall collect any money for any of the purposes aforesaid, shall forfeit any sum not exceeding five pounds, and all and every of the said offences shall be heard and determined in a summary way, before one or more Justice or Justices of the Peace for the county, and the conviction of the same may be had upon oath or oaths of one or more credible witnesses, and the amount of the penalty shall be fixed by such Justice or Justices, but not exceeding the several sums before mentioned; and in case any such penalty shall not be paid, such Justice or Justices, shall, cause the same to be levied by distress and sale of the offender's goods together with all costs attending such distress and sale; and in case no sufficient distress can be had, such Justice or Justices shall, commit the offender to the committing gaol, or some house of correction there to remain, without bail, for any time not exceeding three calendar months, not less than two months.

VI. That all sums of money which at any time heretofore have been paid as a subscription towards any of the purposes prohibited by this Act, and shall, for the space of three months after the passing of this Act, remain undivided in the hands of any Treasurer, &c. or placed out at interest, and all sums of money which shall after the passing this Act, be paid as a subscription or contribution towards any of the purposes prohibited by this Act, shall be forfeited, one moiety thereof to his majesty, and one moiety to such person as shall sue for the same.

VII. And, for the better discovery of the sums of money paid or given in the hands of any Treasurer, &c. for any purpose prohibited by this Act, be it further enacted, That all persons who shall be liable by virtue of this Act to be sued for the same shall be obliged to answer upon oath to any information which shall be perferred against him in any Court of Equity, for discoving the sums of money so paid into the hands of any Treasurer, &c. for any of the purposes aforesaid; and such Court shall make such orders herein, as shall seem just, and no person shall refuse to answer such information.

VIII. That upon payment into the Court, in which such information shall be filed, of all the money, paid or given up by any such Treasurer, &c. and upon making a full discovery of all the securities upon which all such money shall be then placed out, the person paying such money into Court, and making such discovery shall be discharged from all forfeitures and penalties which may have been incurred by him by reason of having collected or received such money, and from all actions and other suits respecting the same.

IX. That all and every person, who shall offend against this Act, shall equally with all other persons, be called upon and compelled to give evidence as a witness on behalf of the pro-

secutor or informer, and that in all such cases
every person having given evidence as aforesaid, shall be free, from any information to be
laid or prosecution to be commenced, against him
for having offended in the matter wherein or
relative to which he shall have given evidence
as aforesaid.

X. That on complaint and information on
oath before any Justice of the Peace, of any offence having been committed against this Act,
such Justice is hereby authorised and required to
summon the person charged with being an offender to appear before such Justice at a certain time and place to be specified; and if
any person or persons so summoned, shall not
appear, then such Justice shall issue his warrant, persons so summoned and bringing
him before such Justice, or it shall be lawful for
such Justice, if he shall think fit, without issuing any previous summons, upon such complaint or information on oath aforesaid, to issue his warrant, for apprehending the person
and bring him before such Justice and upon the
person complained against, appearing upon such
summon, or warrant, before such Justice, then
such justice, shall, and is hereby authorised and
required forthwith, to make enquiry touching
the matters complained of, and to hear and determine the matter of every such complaint,
and upon confession by the party, or proof by
one or more credible witness or witnesses upon
oath, to convict or acquit the party against
whom complaint shall have been made.

XI. And be it further enacted, That it shal
be lawful for the said Justice of the Peace, before

whom any such information shall be made, and he is authorised at the request in writing of any of the parties, to issue a summons to any witness or witnesses, to give evidence before such Justice at the time appointed for hearing and determining such complaint, and which time and place shall be specified in such summons ; and if any person so summoned to appear shall not appear or offer some reasonable excuse for the default, or appearing shall not submit to be examined as a witness, and to give his evidence before such Justice, then it shall be lawful for such Justices by warrant under his or their hand or hands, to commit such person making default in appearing, or appearing and refusing to give evidence, to some prison within the jurisdiction of such Justice, until such person shall submit himself to be examined, and shall give his evidence before such Justice as aforesaid.

XII. That the Justice before whom any person shall be convicted of any offence against this Act, or by whom any person shall be committed to prison for not appearing as a witness, or not submitting to be examined, shall cause all such convictions, and the warrants or order of such commitment, to be drawn up in the form or to the effect set forth in the Schedule to this Act.

XIII. That the Justice before whom any such conviction shall be had, shall cause the same (drawn up in the form or to the effect herein before directed)to be fairly written on parchment, and transmitted to the next General Sessions, or General Quarter Sessions of the Peace to be

holden for the county, riding, &c. wherein such
conviction was had,. to be filed and kept
amongst the Records of the said General Sessions, or General Quarter Sessions; and in case
any person shall appeal, in manner herein-after
mentioned, from the judgment of the said Justice to the said General Sessions, or General
Quarter Sessions, the Justices in such General
Sessions or General Quarter Sessions are required, upon receiving such conviction, to proceed
to the determination of the matter of the said appeal, according to the directions of this Act.

XIV. That if any person convicted of an offence punishable by this Act, shall think himself
aggrieved by the judgment of such Justice or
Justices before whom he shall have been convicted, such person shall have liberty to appeal
from such convictions to the next Court of General Sessions, or General Quarter Sessions of
the Peace, which shall be held for the county,
riding, &c. wherein such offence was committed, and that the execution of every judgment
shall be suspended, in case the person so convicted shall immediately enter into recognizance
before such Justice or Justices with two sufficient sureties, in the penalty of twenty pounds,
upon condition to prosecute such appeal with
effect; the Justices in the said next Courts, are
hereby authorised and required to hear and fi-
nally determine the matter of the said appeal,
and to award such costs as shall appear just, to
be paid by either party, which decision shall be
final; if upon hearing the said appeal, the
judgment of the Justice or Justices before whom

the appellant shall have been convicted, shall be confirmed, such appellant shall immediately be committed by the said Court, either to the common gaol or house of correction, according to such conviction, and for the space of time therein mentioned, without bail, and also until the payment of such costs as shall be awarded by the said Court.

XV. That nothing in this Act contained shall extend, take away, or abridge the powers and authorities given to any Justice of the Peace in and by any Acts of Parliament heretofore made and now in force touching any combinations of any Manufacturers, Journeymen, or Workmen, or for settling and adjusting disputes or differences between Masters and their Journeymen, or the rate or amount of wages to be paid to such Journeymen, the mode or time of their working, or the quantity of work to be done, &c. but that all Justices of the Peace shall continue to execute all the powers and authorities given to them by such Acts of Parliament, in the same manner as they might have done if this Act had not been made.

XVI. That this Act shall not authorise any person carrying on any business, to employ therein any Journeyman or Workman contrary to the regulations contained in any Acts of Parliament which have been heretofore made, and is now in force, for regulating the method of carrying on any particular manufacture, or business, or the work of the persons employed therein, without the previous licence and consent in writing of one of the Justices of the Peace, expressing the reason of granting the same, which licence it shall be lawful for one such Justice to grant, whenever the qualified Journeymen or Workmen usually employed in any manufacture, trade, or business, shall refuse to work therein for reasonable wages, or to work with any particular persons.

XVII. And be it further enacted, That if any action shall be commenced against any person for any thing by him done in pursuance of this Act, such action shall be commenced within three months after the thing done, and shall be laid in the proper county; and the defendant or defendants in such action may plead the general issue, and give the special matter in evidence for his defence; and if upon trial a verdict shall pass for the defendant, or the plaintiff become nonsuited, or discontinue his prosecution, or judgment shall be given against him, then such defendant shall have treble costs awarded to him against such plaintiff.

FINIS.

RULES,

ADOPTED BY THE

JOURNEYMEN

MILLWRIGHTS,

FOR THE

WELL-GOVERNING

OF THEIR

SOCIETY.

LONDON:

PRINTED BY 'G. BALNE, No. 6, WATER-LANE,
FLEET-STREET.

1801.

RULES, &c.

ARTICLE I.

WAGES.

To work for a mafter mill-wright, five fhillings and three-pence per day.

II.

When at work for a gentleman, or company of gentlemen, fix fhillings and three-pence per day.

III.

Any man going to work from the fhop, to have his lodging paid, or time allowed to walk to his work.

IV.

That members of this fociety do work for fuch mafters as are by us deemed legal at this time, April 6, 1801: On the contrary, that members of this fociety fhall

not

not work for any mafter, under the denomination of mill-wrights, engineers, or any
other defcription of men, but fuch as are
deemed legal, both by mafters and men,
from this date, April 6, 1801, except they
receive fix fhillings and three-pence per
day.

V.

All mafters within twenty-five miles of
London, are included in thefe articles.

VI.

Any man going to work under the advanced wages fhall be fined nine-pence per
day, for the time he worked under the faid
wages; the money to be difpofed of as in
article VII.

VII.

Every member, when admitted into this
fociety, fhall pay the fum of two pounds
two fhillings, as entrance money, and
three half-pence per week into the fociety's
funds, which is eftablifhed for the fupport
of fuperannuated and infirm mill-wrights,
who may become the objects of our charity, The objects of our charity to be
chofen

chofen at a general meeting, not exceeding
three in number, to receive four fhillings
per week each, during their natural lives:
A vacancy by the death of one or more of
thefe three, to be filled by fuch as are
approved of at the next general meeting.

VIII.

If any ftranger fhould pay all or part of
his entrance money, during the time he is
allowed to prove his right to the trade,
after which if he fhould be objected to, he
fhall have the whole of the money returned he fo paid.

IX.

Books fhall be kept, containing the
name of every mill-wright who has agreed
to thefe articles; and if any member violate
or infringe upon any of the faid articles,
his name to be noted in the book, and the
violation or infringment, inferted in the
fame.

X.

When in the fhop, members of this fociety to work ten hours for a day, when
daylight will permit; to be entitled to half
an

an hour for breakfaft, one hour for dinner, and half an hour at four o'clock, for watering time, from the 13th of February to the 9th of November. One half of the dinner-hour, and the half hour at four o'clock, to be difcontinued, from the 9th of November to the 13th of February. When extra time is made, two hours and a half to be confidered the firft quarter of a day, one hour the fecond quarter, and fo in proportion for any longer period of time. For every night's work, to be allowed two days, likewife two days for Sunday : Meal times, and watering times, to be taken the fame as in day-work.

XI.

When out from the fhop at work, members of this fociety, to work nine hours and a half for a day, when day-light will permit; to be entitled to half an hour for breakfaft, half an hour at eleven o'clock, one hour for dinner, and half an hour at four o'clock for watering time, from the 13th of February to the 9th of November. The half-hour a four o'clock only to be difcon-

difcontinued from the 9th of November to
the 13th of February. When extra time
is made, two hours to be confidered the
firft quarter of a day, one hour the fecond
quarter, and fo in proportion for any
longer period of time: for every night's
work to be allowed two days; likewife two
days for Sundays: meal times and watering
times to be taken the fame as in day-work.

XII.

To prevent impofition for the future, no
perfon can be admitted a member of this
fociety from the date hereof, July 5, 1797,
to July 5, 1804, except he has ferved a
legal apprenticefhip of five years, and
worked feven years from the date of his
indentures: And at the expiration of the
term, 1804, no man can be confidered
eligible, without producing an indenture for
the full term of feven years, except the
fenior fon of a mill-wright, who ferved the
term of feven years to his father, without
the form of an indenture. And every
man fhall be allowed one week for every
hundred

hundred miles diſtance he may have to apply to procure his indenture.

XIII.

Every member to pay one ſhilling per week for each week he has work'd from the expiration of his term of years, as ex-preſſed by his indenture, to the comple-tion of his term of ſeven years; the ſaid money to be paid at two ſhillings and ſix-pence per week into the hands of ſome of his ſhopmates where he is employed, un-til the money required be all paid. But ſhould any member leave his place of em-ployment, prior to the ſaid money being paid, he ſhall receive a written acknow-ledgment from the perſon who has received the money, in part paid, which he muſt produce at his next place of employment, and ſo on until his arrears be made good.

XIV.

No perſon ſhall be admitted as a legal apprentice ſubſequent to his attaining the ſixteenth year of his age.

XV.

The ſociety's money ſhall be depoſited in the public funds.

XVI.

A committee of eleven members shall be chosen out of the society, by ballot, to dispose of the said money, and concert upon such other business as the society shall transmit or lay before them: And seven members of the said committee shall be sufficient to form a quorum.

XVII.

The committee shall be permanent six months, and meet every two months; each member shall be allowed the sum of one shilling on their meeting-day or night, likewise his loss of time, at the rate of five shillings and three-pence per day, with other necessary expences.

XVIII.

Any member of this society refusing to act in the committee, after being legally chosen, shall pay the fine of five shillings.

XIX.

All grievances, complaints, or any other business appertaining to this society, shall be delivered in writing.

XX.

XX.

Every member belonging to the committee, on going out of office, shall make good his accounts at the general meeting on which he is replaced, or in default thereof shall pay double the sum or sums of money he is deficient; and if any member belonging to the said committee, shall absent himself from the general meeting on which he goes out of office, he shall pay the fine of five shillings.

XXI.

Any member of the committee, who shall absent himself from the ordinary or extraordinary meetings, without being able to give his brother members satisfactory reasons, shall pay the fine of two shillings and six-pence.

XXII.

If any member enter the committee-room in a state of intoxication he shall be fined one shilling, and ordered to withdraw, in non-compliance with the said order, he shall fine two shillings and six-pence, and if any member behave disorderly, or swear,

or

or ufe any obfcene language during the time the bufinefs is tranfacting, he fhall for every fuch offence be fined fix-pence.

XXIII.

Whoever fhall refufe to make good his payments, or act contrary to any eftablifh-ed rules belonging to this fociety, fo that his fhopmates are under the neceffity of leaving their employ through him, fhall not be acknowledged (after fuch an act) as a member of this foeiety, until he has made good all lofs of time to the fatisfac-tion of the party or parties fo injured, by being out of work.

XXIV.

WORK DONE BY THE PIECE.

Wheel-patterns, below two feet diame-ter, not exceeding five inches wide in the rim, to be nineteen fhillings per foot dia-meter ; wheel-patterns, two feet diameter, exceeding five inches wide in the rim, twenty fhillings per foot diameter ; wheel-patterns above two feet diameter, not ex-ceeding five inches wide in the rim, eigh-teen fhillings per foot diameter ; wheel-

patterns,

patterns above two feet diameter, exceeding five inches in the rim, nineteen fhillings per foot diameter.

XXV.

Caft-iron wheels. — To chip fourteen
fuperficial inches for one fhilling, when the
journeyman finds chifels and files; to chip
fixteen fuperficial inches for one fhilling,
when the mafter finds chifels and files.

XXVI.

French ftones.—Making ftones the flat
way of the burr, one pound four fhillings
per foot diameter; if edge way of the burr,
one pound eight fhillings per foot diameter; if end way of the burr, two pounds
fixteen fhillings per foot diameter.

FINIS.

Printed by G. Balne, Water-Lane, Fleet-Street.

FACTS

and

OBSERVATIONS,

TO PROVE THE

IMPOLICY and DANGEROUS TENDENCY,

OF THE

BILL

NOW BEFORE PARLIAMENT,

For limiting the number of Apprentices, and other Restrictions

in the

CALICO PRINTING BUSINESS.

Together with a Concise History

OF THE

Combination of the Journeymen.

MANCHESTER.

PRINTED BY J. ASTON, 84, DEANSGATE

A FEW
PLAIN OBSERVATIONS,
&c.

THAT which is morally wrong, cannot be politically right, was the sentiment of a great statesman, as delivered in the British House of Commons : in other words, that which is wrong in principle, can never be right in practice. If we apply this to the question now before parliament, respecting the disputes between the masters and the journeymen calico printers, we shall, in the first place, be led to consider how far it is consistent with justice and sound policy, for the Legislature to impose any law for the government of manufactories. The best writers on this subject agree, and experience has fully proved, that all attempts to give laws to manufactures, are erroneous in their principles, and injurious in their effects ; the best of these writers appears to be Adam Smith, whose opinion I believe is universally allowed to be sufficient authority. In his enquiry into the nature and cause of the wealth of nations, he has clearly proved the impolicy of corporation or parliamentary laws in directing the labours of manufactures, he says*—" All systems either of preference or restraint, " being completely taken away, the obvious and simple

* Third Vol. Book 4th. Page 42, Wealth of Nations.

" system of natural liberty establishes itself, of its own ac-
" cord. Every man as long as he does not violate the laws
" of justice, is left perfectly free to pursue his own interest,
" in his own way; and to bring both his own industry and
" capital into competition with those of any other man, or
" order of men. The sovereign is completely discharged
" from a duty, in the attempting to perform which, he
" must always be exposed to innumerable delusions, and
" for the proper performance of which, no human wisdom
" or knowledge could be sufficient, *viz.* The duty of su-
" perintending the industry of private people, and of di-
" recting it towards the employment most suitable to the
" interest of the society." With respect to limiting by
law the number of journeymen, apprentices, or any other
description of workmen to be employed in any manufacto-
ry; it is injurious both to masters and servants. With respect to the servant being denied the liberty of working at
what he thinks proper, the same author observes*—" The
" property which every man has in his own labour, as it is
" the original foundation of all other property, so it is the
" most sacred and inviolable. The patrimony of a poor
" man, lies in the strength and dexterity of his hands, and
" to hinder him from employing this strength and dexte-
" rity, in what manner he thinks proper, without injury to
" his neighbour, is a plain violation of this most sacred
" property." And it is injurious to the masters also, he
adds—" As it hinders the one from working at what he
" thinks proper, so it hinders the other from employing
" whom they think proper; to judge whether he is fit to be
" employed, may surely be trusted to the discretion of the
" employer, whose interest it so much concerns. The
" affected anxiety of the law-giver lest he should employ an

5

" improper person, is evidently as impertinent as it is
" oppressive."

But if we consider the nature of the calico-print business,
as being entirely a fancy trade, and subject to the continual
changes of fashion, we see still more the utter impossibility of
fixing the number or description of persons to be employed,
or the exact proportion of journeymen or apprentices. It
however may be observed that the print business, affords as much common easy work for apprentices, as the
weaving business, which may generally employ nearer three
apprentices to one journeyman, than three journeymen to
one apprentice, which I understand is the unreasonable
proportion the journeymen printers wish to have fixed by
law. If parliament should adopt the unwise principle of
interfering in the government of Manufactures, and fix the
proportion of apprentices to be employed, as the journeymen printers wish, the consequence would be, that great
numbers of journeymen would be employed at common
work which belongs to the apprentices only. Can it be supposed reasonable for a journeyman weaver to be employed in weaving coarse goods, the work of an apprentice, and to have as much for weaving a coarse piece
of fifty threads per inch, as for a fine cambric of one hundred and fifty threads per inch. If this be thought unreasonable, the same will exactly apply to printers; for in the
print business, apprentices can only be employed at common
easy work, which deserves a much less price, and should
not be given to journeymen.*

The partial effect of the evil just mentioned is now felt
for the want of apprentices, and in some cases the journeymen are now receiving a shilling for easy work, that might

* By the experience of above 400 years, says Dr. Burn, it seems time to lay aside all
endeavours to bring under strict regulations, what, in its own nature seems incapable of
minute limitation, for if all persons in the same kind of work were to receive equal wages, there would be no emulation, and no room left for industry or ingenuity.

be done by an apprentice for fourpence. This limitation of apprentices, necessarily destroys the reasonable division of labour, which is so useful in every art; the great advantage of which is so clearly explained in Smith's Wealth of Nations in the most simple trades, viz. that of manufacturing pins and nails, the truth of which is generally proved every day in all the manufactures in the kingdom. If the journeymen printers do not wish to destroy this necessary division of labour; why all this anxiety about apprentices, who only can be employed at common work, which naturally belongs to them? and why prevent by law, apprentices being taken, if it is notorious, as the journeymen state, that there are now more in the trade than can be employed? But this appears to be wholly incorrect, by numerous persons still wishing to become apprentices. The truth is, the journeymen from a mistaken policy, have long since formed themselves into a combination. The origin and progress of which will appear in the paper subjoined.

The existence of this combination, was sufficiently proved to the committee of the House of Commons, when they first presented their petition; and though many of the more sober, and wiser journeymen, are now convinced of the injustice and very bad effects of this combination, and wish the trade to be left to its natural liberty, yet other journeymen, either from their private interest, as managers of this combination, or from an ignorance of their true interests, continue to trouble the trade, and the legislature, with their unfounded complaints as will be shortly more fully proved. The bill they wish to obtain, embraces only one object, that of preventing masters from taking apprentices. From the extent and complicated nature of the business, this may appear strange, but when the power

of their combination is known, it will be accounted for.
By their combination they prevent the master employing
any journeyman they do not approve of, who as *they say*
is not a fair man; and all journeymen must ask the constable of the shop, for the time being, (an officer appointed
by the combination) for work, before they ask the master.
They can discharge a journeyman from service without his
master's consent; they can advance their wages, and in
many instances, prevent the master from making reasonable
abatements for spoiled work. While they are all at work,
they prevent the master taking more apprentices than they
approve of, and such a number, as the nature of the work
requires. In any case, when the master does not shew a
readiness to comply with their commands, they order both
journeymen and apprentices, to *strike, and turn out* (as
they term it,) and leave their work, in this situation. The
masters have often been thus deserted, and having empty
shops, they have been under the necessity, either of submitting to their unreasonable demands, or of taking on, and
teaching new hands, the last of which, some of the masters
have preferred. This is the only remedy the master has now
left and the journeymen wish to deprive him of it, by the
bill in question. If it be said, the master has, or may have,
the advantage of the law against combination, it is true;
but this affords him no recompence, for the loss of his trade,
while his workmen are maintained in idleness, by subscriptions from the members of this combination, through the
trade at large, and to grant the journeymen printers the
object of their bill, would be to give them, the power of
strengthening and completing their dangerous combination,
and deprive the masters of the only remedy left them. It
is true, that the well-being of the labouring part of the community, ought to claim the attention of Government, and
of every wise and good subject; but at the same time care

should be taken to do justice to all, and this will be best done by protecting our liberties and property at home, and opening markets abroad for our manufactures. Both masters and servants must always be subject to the changes and inconveniences occasioned by war, and other political events; and even husbandmen are dependant on the weather, and the mutability of the seasons. These evils cannot be cured by any restrictive laws, imposed on arts and manufactures.

The journeymen printers' situation is much better than many working people in other trades, it appeared from accounts taken from the books of fourteen of the principal masters, when the journeymen first presented their petition, that the highest wages paid to any one journeyman employed by these fourteen masters, was 103*l*. 5*s*. 3*d*. per annum; that the lowest was 51*l*. 12*s*. 10*d*. per annum, and that the whole wages paid to all the journeymen employed by these fourteen houses, averaged per man for three years 1*l*. 8*s*. 3½*d* per week, so that if it is possible for a journeyman to get 103*l*. 5*s*. 3*d*. per annum, no one can reasonably suppose that they have any occasion to complain, especially when it is considered that their daily labour is only ten hours and a quarter in summer, and from seven to eight hours in the winter.

It is a fact, that there are now many masters in the trade, and carrying on much business, who were enabled to begin by a capital they acquired by the good wages they earned while journeymen. The wisest part of the journeymen are free to confess, that they have suffered most from the combination. The large sums of money paid for the support of men in idleness, whom they have ordered to *turn out*, to force the masters to submit to their demands, has been the principal cause of their poverty, and has often reduced them to want. This would not have been the case, had they not found means to prevent those journeymen from getting work in the trade who did not wish to submit to their laws. These men found themselves under the necessity, either of submitting to the rules of the combination, or of leaving the business, and it too often happens that the most ignorant part of workmen, forms the majority. But from past experience many are weary of the combination, that were formerly advocates for it, and would be glad the business should be suffered to take its natural course.

The partial and unnatural method of preventing the masters from taking apprentices, has already been found injurious to the trade, and if an act passes to destroy this liberty of the masters, the consequence will be the general decay of the trade; for as the taking of apprentices has enabled the masters to encrease the business, and to make it one of the most prosperous, and productive trades in the kingdom, so the taking away, or any way limiting this right of the masters, would decrease and destroy the business, or drive it to a country where it might enjoy full liberty.

But it may be useful to shew how such a measure would immediately operate against the interest of the journeymen, the masters, the different manufacturers connected with the print business, and the country at large.—First the journeymen themselves; It is a certain fact, that the restraining of masters from taking apprentices, has induced many to print greater quantities of single colours, on machines, than they otherwise would have done; this contracts and limits taste and fancy, and prevents a greater variety of work from being introduced into the business, which deprives the journeymen of much work, for want of apprentices to do plain and easy work at a moderate expence. Chintz patterns, of six or eight colours which afford much work for the journeymen, could not be executed on account of the great expence; and this restraint would lessen the sale of prints, by lessening the variety, and force a simple style of work of one and two colours, that might be done principally by machines; thus the journeymen, instead of gaining, would lose by such a measure.

Secondly, The masters would be much injured by such a measure. They have laid out not less than two millions in establishing works, for the accommodation of the business, and if the trade be thus injured, their loss will be immense; while the general effect would completely subvert the relation of master and servant, in placing the former under the slavish controul of the latter.

Thirdly, Those workmen connected with, and dependant upon the print trade, would sustain a great loss. If we take the printers to be 7,000, * the number that signed the petition, we may reckon three persons to each printer, employed in the print works, making in the whole 21,000. Every printer will employ nine weavers to make the cloth he prints; now supposing the printer to print three pieces per day, and the weaver to weave two pieces per week, the number will be 63,000. These 63,000 weavers, will employ 25,000 persons in making the yarns ready for the loom. According to this calculation, it appears, that there are 109,000 persons dependent on the 7,000 printers, so that every printer set to work, will employ nearly 16 persons in all the different branches of the cotton business. I have before stated that great quantities of single colours are now printed by machines, but should the fashion abroad and at home change, and instead of single colours done by machines, our customers should want patterns from 3 to 7 colours done by printers only, they would require near one half more than there are now in the trade. What would the con-

---

We take these *data* from a petition to the House of Commons presented by the journeymen calico printers, who estimated themselves at 7,000 But we have some reason to suppose they included in that number the designers, and the block cutters, which supposing to be 2,000, then tha calculation which follows must be reduced accordingly.

sequence be, if the masters could not take apprentices ? Either our markets for printed calicoes would only be half supplied, and one half of our weavers would be deprived of work, or one half of the calicoes now printed would be sold in the white, for want of workmen to print them.

From the foregoing statement it will not be contended but that the increase of the print-business is of great importance to the country at large, and government had better give premiums for apprentices than prevent them being taken, and more especially if we take into consideration, the great revenue it raises to government. The present duty on printed calicoes is about 6s. 3d. per piece, taking an average of the cloths; and supposing one printer to print three pieces per day, the revenue arising from this one printer, will be 292*l*. 10s. per annum, and supposing 7,000 printers to be employed, will produce 2,047,500*l* per annum.

But the bill itself could not be applied without great confusion : suppose, for instance, that a master takes into his employ, thirty journeymen, and he is allowed by act of parliament only to take ten apprentices, has them bound to him by legal indentures, but his trade afterwards falls off, and he is under the necessity of discharging half the number of his journeymen, can he in this case discharge his apprentices ? or so many of them, as will reduce them to the number allowed by law for the journeymen he employs, when at the same time he has bound himself by indenture, to keep the apprentices, find them constant work, and teach them their trade. If he is only to keep his 30 journeymen until he gets his number of apprentices bound, and may then discharge the journeymen, the bill would have no effect, and if he discharges the apprentices with the journeymen, it would be a breach of his covenants, and the apprentices might take the advantage of the law against him. On these views of the subject, it is clear, that such a bill would deprive masters and servants of their just rights, would be attended with great difficulties in its application, and in its consequences destroy the trade, deprive the journeymen, and a great part of the population of the country of work; decrease the revenue, and injure the nation at large. If this bill be suffered to exist under any modification, the principle is admitted, and a most dangerous precedent established, and if so, a door well be opened to applications from all descriptions of artizans, mechanics, and even day-labourers; and why should not masters present petitions to the House of Commons, for bills to regulate the number of masters: and not to suffer above a certain number to enter into business, and to prevent those already in the trade, from being injured? This might be done with equal justice and necessity, but every one would see the impolicy and folly of it. It is to be hoped that the Legislature will see the wisdom and necessity of making a public declaration, that they will leave the manufactures to their natural liberty, and thus prevent similar applications by which they would be continually harrassed. Nothing can be more pleasant to the heart of a good man, than to better the condition of the poor; and I am confident that the course I have just mentioned, is the most likely to secure constant work, good wages, peace and comfort to the journeymen, and prosperity to the whole trade.

The HISTORY

THE HISTORY

OF THE

Combination of the Journeymen Calico Printers.

To give the History of this combination, it will be necessary to premise that the printing business of this kingdom
was originally carried on in and about London ; it afforded
the masters great profits, and the servants high wages, there
being little competition.   The Londoners had it to themselves : they had no corporation laws, yet they made use of
all possible means to keep the business to themselves. When
the Lancashire people began to print, the general cry
among the London journeymen was, that the trade would
be ruined by the Country printers doing their work so cheap.
The printers in Lancashire however kept encreasing their
business, principally by apprentices, and found the demand
for their goods more than equal the increase of their work
Messrs. Peels had made a considerable progress in the business which the Londoners beheld with an envious eye.
When Messrs. Livesey, Hargreaves and Co. began to print
at Mosney near Preston, this house took in a partner of the
name of Smith, who had learned the business with the old-
est printer then living in London, Mr. Stephen Williams.
Mr. Smith, on joining Messrs. Livesey and Co. wishing to
have the work done well, engaged a number of the London
journeymen to work in Lancashire, about the year 1783; and
to this time we are to look for the beginning of that extensive combination which has caused so much trouble in the
business of calico printing.   So soon as these *gentlemen
journeymen* (for they had more the appearance of gentlemen
than workmen) got down into the Country, they assumed
(as coming from London) a great degree of consequence,

and making great professions of skill and ingenuity in the business, the acting partners, at Messrs. Livesey and Co's. works, who knew little of the nature of the business, were easily duped by them, and gave them most extravagant wages, and as these journeymen had so long complained of the Country people doing their work low, their great object was to advance wages, and to keep them as high in the Country as in London, and in consequence, this house had such sums of money to pay in wages, that they were under the necessity of keeping persons constantly collecting Cash in different parts of the Country; but this was not the worst, so ill disposed were these journeymen to the Country masters, that they executed their work in a very imperfect manner, and would often tell the over-looker, when he complained of bad work, that it was good enough for the Country. I have been informed some of them actually burnt their pieces, to avoid abatements for spoiled work. Such a system of extravagance and plunder, was perhaps never before carried on by any number of workmen in the kingdom.

Though this house had hurt itself by speculations, yet this was the principal cause of its ruin; for though the execution of their work cost such enormous sums of ready money, yet it was so imperfectly done, they were constantly pushing the markets with quantities of spoiled work, which they often sold for less than the price of the cloth and amount of the duty. This soon brought the house into an embarassed situation. The acting partners now attempted to lessen the expence of the work by means of machinery and apprentices, but the journeymen, who to prevent the use of machinery and the taking of apprentices, entered into a combination, "*turned out*" and succeeded in taking from their work the apprentices also, for the purpose of enforcing their demands. This happened I believe in the year 1785 or 1786, and was the first *turn out* in the print trade in Lancashire, called the " Mosney turn out." The name of the manager of this combination was Walker, who under the specious pretence of serving the trade, went round the different print grounds, to collect money to support the men out of work.

During this time, Messrs. Livesey and Co. were under the necessity of trying various methods of printing by machinery to their great loss.—Journeymen on the other hand, vowed they would either break their masters, or make them submit to their terms: but after a struggle of upwards of three months, the workmen at the other print grounds began to think their cause a bad one, and having reason to believe, that the manager of this combination who pretended so much concern for the good of the trade, was embezzling their money they left off subscribing, the consequence of which was, the Mosney workmen, were under the necessity of going to work on their masters' terms. Messrs. Livesey and Co. now did better work than ever they did before: being in some degree masters of their workmen. But having lost their capital, they were not able to pay their bills in London, and in May 1788, they stopped payment, after having spent near half a million of money.

The print trade after this failure, took a favourable turn, and the masters, by the end of the year 1788, had taken into their employ nearly the whole of these men; but as many of them were men of the worst principles and conduct, it would have been greatly to the advantage of the Masters, and the trade in general, had these men been kept from the different print grounds, for no sooner did they get to work, than they began to disseminate their old principles, and as they were now scattered all over the Trade, they had a better opportunity than before, of forming a general combination.

Their specuous pretences of serving the trade and bettering

the condition of the workmen, soon gained over to them, the unthinking many, they however proceeded by degrees; they at first established a fund by small monthly contributions, which they called a " fund for the relief of sick members," but which was really intended for other purposes,*viz*. the support of turn-outs, as appears from a note affixed to their articles, a copy of whioh came into the hands of the masters. The trade in 1789 went on well, and workmen were much wanted,a greater opportunity was therefore given them, of forwarding their new combination which they did, by holding regular meetings in different parts of the country, for the purpose of forming plans for collecting money. Walker,who was the chief manager of the Mosney turn-out, often presided as chairman at their Meetings. They had now regular articles for the regulation of the society, at the beginning of which they stated their intentions were to prevent persons from becoming masters who were ignorant of the business, and to set those who were already, or might become masters, more on a level with each other, to prevent the increase of hands, advance the wages, and diminish the number of working hours.—Many however of the most conscientious journeymen, stood out for a long time, rather than act so contrary to their duty and the interest of their masters. But finding the power of this combination so great, they chose rather to submit, than be obliged to leave their employ. Almost at every meeting they made laws which operated as fresh impositions on their masters, and more officers were appointed for enforcing the laws ; and, this at a time when the demand for goods was so great, and workmen so much wanted, that premiums were given for them by the masters to the amount of 5, 10, and 15 guineas per man, so untrue are the assertions of the men, that distress and want of work, has been the cause of this combination, that the reverse has been the fact; they have al-

ways been most dissatisfied, when they have had the most
work and greatest wages. The combination being thus generally established, their high wages enabled them to sub-
scribe more largely to their fund, and they applied their
laws with greater severity ; this caused some of the masters
to throw off the yoke ; amongst whom were the house of
Messrs Roe and Kershaw of Chadkirk near Stockport, the
greatest part of their workmen however turned out, and
were supported from the journeymen's fund, and the masters
were under the necessity of continuing their business by
means of new hands.

The power of the combination continued still to increase as
well as their fund, they now levied fines, from 5 to 15 guineas
upon any journeyman that disobeyed their orders whom they
called, *knob-sticks* ; both the masters and workmen were now
completely at the controul of this combination ; few apprentices were taken, and for every one they permitted their
masters to take, they demanded 5 guineas premium, either
from the master or apprentice, which they put to their general fund. But that which was found more grievous to the
masters, was the premiums given to the journeymen, which
tempted the men to leave their employ, with their work unfinished, often in debt, and without a day's notice. This
caused a meeting to be called of the masters, early in the
year 1790, at the Bridgewater Arms Manchester, to take
into consideration the state of the trade, and to adopt measures to defeat and prevent the unlawful combinations of the
journeymen. To prevent masters from enticing each other's
men by premiums ; and to cause the men to finish up their
work and not to leave their masters in debt, it was agreed
that each master should give his servant when he left his employ lawfully, a written discharge, and that no master should
employ another's servant, who had not with him such a discharge, purporting that he had finished his work, and left
his master honourably. To counteract this, and keep up
the practice of getting premiums from their masters, to

keep up the combination and prevent the masters from applying their new regulations, the greater part of the journeymen and apprentices turned out, which was called the "*General turn-out*,"—when the country was in great confusion. In the day-time, these men held meetings in woods and on commons, and drank and revelled in public houses at night. Hand-bills were published by them, stating very unjustly, that their masters had oppressed them, and that they had overstocked the trade with apprentices, when in fact there were not a sufficient number of journeymen and apprentices in the business. Some of the masters proceeded against a few of the leaders of the combination, by a course of law, but this had no influence on the great body of the men. Having been out a month or six weeks, and the demand for goods being very great, some of the masters agreed to employ their men again on their own terms ; but other houses were determined to be masters of their own business, and direct their own works.

The late Mr. Peel, the father of the family now in business, and who we may call the father of the print business in Lancashire, who had suffered much by the riots of the weavers, against the improvements made in cotton machinery some years before, saw in this combination, the same spirit and the same object pursued, he therefore acted as a friend to improvements and to the interests of his Country, by strongly opposing them: he and other masters now began to supply their empty shops with new hands and apprentices. Sir Rt. Peel who in this business, and the different branches of the cotton business connected with it, has done so much for the interest of his Country, by increasing its resource ; and employing its population also, saw and felt the injurous effects of this combination in Lancashire, and was under the necessity at this time of establishing print works at Tamworth in Staffordshire, where free from the restraints and controul of this combination, has since printed from 40 to 50,000 pieces per annum, principally by means of machinery and apprentices. So soon as the masters appeared to act independently, a few of the journeymen and old apprentices returned to their employment, but they were much abused by those who remained out, and who called themselves *flints*, at the same time stigmatizing the persons who had returned to their work, with the name of *knobsticks*.

The masters now publickly offered the men out of work, their old wages and to continue them the same, but the men declared *wages were not their object*, which was to compel the masters to comply with their laws and regulations; in fact nothing would satisfy them but having the power and dominion. Their fund of money was now applied to support them in a state of idleness, and many of them who had tasted its sweets in the " Mosney turn-out " had no inclination to return to their work. The masters continued to encrease their new workmen, and found those they had taken on at first improved so much, that in the space of two months, they became very useful. Others of the men seeing this, returned to their duty, and the masters engaged not to lower their wages which they had before offered to all the men.

The masters were now enabled to do a tolerable quantity of good work, and the men out of employ finding their money rather low, wished to make an agreement with their masters, and had several meetings with them for that purpose; they at first wished to compromise the business by giving up their most extraordinary demands, that of the masters not being suffered to use machinery &c. they wished the masters to discharge their new apprentices also who had served them in their time of need, but the masters resolved to keep them on, and to manage their business without being controuled by their servants, at the same time gave them liberty to return to their duty. Still promising their old wages. Having now been out upwards of four months, and their fund exhausted, they all returned to their work on their masters' terms, after expending near 5000*l*. besides the loss of their labour which might amount to 10,000*l*. more.

During this *turn out* the masters had taken upwards of two hundred apprentices, yet there was *full work for all*, both new and old, a fact which fully disproves the assertion of the journeymen as a pretence for their conduct, viz. " that the trade was over stocked with hands." The trade now continued quiet and peaceable for some years, until they had recruited their funds, and made good the losses they had sustained in the late *turn-out*; they then again manifested a a spirit of dissaffection, and though the masters had not lowered their wages, they advanced step by step, until the combination had again acquired its full power, and in some instances more than before, for they forced some masters to discharge overlookers and foremen whom the journeymen did not approve of; remembering however, that the " general turn-out" had not been attended with success, they adopted a new plan, that of turning out from one shop at a time, and thus compelling masters, individually, to submit to their laws. The first principal *turn-out* of this sort, which continued for any length of time, was at Messrs. Shaw & Cos. Works, at Ratcliffe near Manchester; its duration was near four months. This house had taken on many journeymen at the " general turn-out," who now received from these journeymen, evil for good, but after both masters and men had expended large sums of money, in a fruitless contest, the men went to work again nearly on their own terms. At other grounds, they found it more difficult to gain their ends; for the trouble they gave their masters, inclined many to make great improvements in machinery, by means of which great quantities of goods were printed, independent of the journeymen; and on their turning out, some masters took on apprentices, and the combination labouring under this last difficulty, in enforcing its commands, now applies to parliament for an act to prevent masters from taking apprentices. Such has been the rise and progress of the combination of the journeymen calico printers.

FINIS.

Aston, Printer.

AN

IMPARTIAL ACCOUNT

OF THE LATE PROCEEDINGS

OF THE

S E A M E N

OF THE

PORT OF TYNE.

BY A. TAR.

Would you hear a tale of woe,
    Listen to our SEAMEN's wrongs;
Gallia is no more our foe,
    BRITAIN *starves her gallant Sons! ! !*

Want with all her ghastly train
    Rushes on our brave in war,
Misery with her iron chain
    Binds each brave and hardy TAR.

x

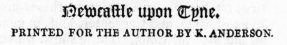

x

x

𝕹𝖊𝖜𝖈𝖆𝖘𝖙𝖑𝖊 𝖚𝖕𝖔𝖓 𝕿𝖞𝖓𝖊.

PRINTED FOR THE AUTHOR BY K. ANDERSON.

1815.

𝔍mpartial 𝔄ccount,

&c. &c.

THE late dispute between the ship-owners
and the seamen of this and the neighbouring
ports having given rise to many erroneous assertions, as an impartial spectator, the author of
this pamphlet undertakes to detail, for the public perusal, the most important circumstances
that occurred both at their public and private
meetings.

In the month of September last, a calulation
was made of the number of seamen out of employment in the ports of Newcastle and
Shields, many of them having large families,
unprovided for, as every vessel in and belonging to the port was already *manned ;* and as
great numbers daily flocking home from the
different ships of war that were then paying
off, and also from the transports, the prospect was rendered very discouraging. The
ship owners were daily binding apprentices,
and it is a rare chance to find ships of two
hundred tons with less than five or six apprentices on board ; in addition to these, are the
Master, Mate, and Carpenter, and, in general,
an old man for Cook. Those ships, which are
the general burden out of this port, seldom
carry more than ten or eleven hands altoge-

ther, although it is well known they are greatly
insufficient to manage the vessels. It is too
much the custom with the ship-owners, when
they bind a stout lad, (who perhaps never saw
the sea in his life) to unship one of the best
seamen, trusting that lad to do the duty of an
experienced sailor, who even in the finest weather is sea-sick for months, and in bad weather
is always to be found below ; yet such is the
natural propensity to *gain*, that the lives of the
rest on board are never thought of; (the ship being well insured, so that the owners cannot loss.)
Finding themselves thus neglected and left to
starve, after having fought their country's battles in the most remote Corners of the world ;
after having shed their blood to secure the
persons and property of the very men who
now refuse them employment, what were
they to do ? They dreaded to enter their
houses where a loving wife and children were
imploring for bread, which they knew not
where to obtain : every foot they heard was
imagined to be that of a ravenous creditor,
seeking payment for the few necessaries of life
they had supplied to keep miserable existence
in being : to beg, they knew not the way ; for
every one who is acquainted with the heart of
a sailor, must be conscious that he is too
proud, even in the greatest distress, to solicit
for charity. When it is said, he is too proud,
let not the Public mistake ; his pride is not
like that of other classes,—his pride is to suffer the greatest privations, rather than seek

pecuniary relief; his pride is in relieving those whom he sees in distress; and to such a pitch will he extend his liberality, that in many instances he has been known to forget that to-morrow he would himself be in need of the very penny he was distributing to his suffering fellow-creatures: thus we know they are not possessed of that want of feeling which has too widely spread itself over our country; nor with that humiliating spirit which is so frequently observed among other classes of the community. Inured to the severest hardships and dangers from childhood; rudely tost about on the bitter face of the ocean, the sailor has not the opportunity of learning the smooth whining cant of the world: heedless of every care, we see him brave the greatest dangers with steady perseverance, even in the prospect of certain death!

The greater part of the sailors having been several months out of employment, and their friends no longer able to support or assist them, they at first collected together in a small body, and consulted each other what was best to be done; and as their numbers were continually increasing, in a few days they agreed to have daily musters to devise some plan to alleviate their growing misery. Finding these meetings were doing nothing towards their obtaining employment, as every ship had the usual complement, they determined that every man should share one fate, and proceeded to un-man all the ships in the harbour. At first they

met with opposition by the different crews;
but they soon became too strong for any single
ship's company to encounter them, and those
who dared to stay on board were made a public example of, by being tarred and feathered;
or if their crime did not amount to that punishment, they had their jackets turned, faces
blacked, and were marched through the town.
By such proceedings, the ships were prevented
from getting to sea, and it was expected by
them the ship-owners would have been induced
to employ extra men in every ship: in this,
however, they were disappointed. The next
plan was to take out the Mates and Carpenters, and oblige them to muster with them;
by which conduct they fully expected to bring
the ship-owners to their terms; but this
scheme proving unsuccessful, they drew out
a scale in what manner the ships should be
manned; this scale was forwarded from Shields
to Newcastle, Sunderland, Hartley, and Blyth,
which was agreed upon by the different majo-
rities of seamen, and presented to the ship-
owners. The scale was for every ship to be
manned according to the transport act, carrying five men and one boy to every hundred
tons burden. The ship-owners now called a
general meeting, at the Northumberland Arms,
North Shields, and agreed that a committee of
the shipping interest should be appointed to
see the ships well manned, without stating any
number of men they were to carry. To this
the seamen would not agree, being bent upon

having their own proposals complied with; they accordingly placed watches on the river in boats, and patroles in the streets to prevent any from going on board; the seamen next called a general meeting of the before-mentioned ports to assemble on Cullercoat sands, each party carrying the British flag at their head, to shew their attachment to their King and Country; each party then formed a ring by themselves, and were addressed by thirteen men chosen by the body to transact any business that might be requisite; after the men's names had been called over, they formed a large ring of between eight and nine thousand men, the different men chosen stood in the middle, and were sworn as follows:

" We swear to be true to our good old King George the Third, and the Constitution, and never to forsake each other in the cause we are now engaged in, to walk peaceably and quietly about our business at all times; and never to set foot on board any ship to work until this most important business is settled."

After they were all sworn the whole body gave three cheers, and each division marched to their respective homes. Vessels of every description were now prevented from going to sea, by boats and crews appointed for that purpose, while regular watches patroled the streets. Several of the men being in the greatest distress, those who were able subscribed

towards their relief; this, however, was found
to be inadequate to the demands made; it was
then thought necessary to allow small vessels
to go to sea, belonging to Scotland and ports
to the southward of Sunderland, on paying ten
shillings for each man on board, to support
those in distress on shore. Vessels going to
Foreign Ports also paid their quota; ships
laden with King's Stores, bound to London,
and Newcastle Traders, were allowed to sail,
on paying twenty shillings per man. By these
means, any man wanting relief made application at the General Musters, and it was determined by the majority what each man was to
receive. The money paid by Masters of ships
was given to certain men, appointed for that
purpose, and every day what was received and
expended, was made known to the whole.—
These men, as before mentioned, were chosen
by the Body, and when once chosen, it was
needless to endeavor getting clear. So strict
were their laws, and so firmly attended to, that
any man refusing to transact his part, he was
blacked and put on a tree, for public example.
The following Articles were made at the beginning : viz.—

ARTICLE I. Finding so many Seamen out of employment, and
in great distress, we have altogether agreed not to go on board any
ship or vessel, until every man can be provided for; to certify which,
we individually sign our names to the annexed list, paying one penny, as an acknowledgment to the same.

II. It is expected, every man will meet at any time and place the
majority of Seamen shall think fit to appoint.

III. Every man missing his muster, shall pay sixpence the first time; one shilling the second; and the third time he shall be tarred and feathered.

IV. If any man shall be found on board of ship after he has been taken out, or has been joined to this Body; he shall have his jacket turned, his face blacked, and marched through the town; if found again on board, he shall be tarred and feathered.

V. If any man shall tell the names of any of the men appointed to transact business, he shall suffer such punishment as the Seamen at large shall think fit.

VI. If any man shall be known to divulge the proceedings of this Body, he shall be tarred and feathered.

VII. As it is most likely the Owners will find out some of the men during the business, and afterwards will not employ them, it is expected every man will contribute to their support after this business is settled, by paying the sum of two shillings each, per voyage, until they get employment.

VIII. Should any man be taken and confined during the business, he is to be supported by the majority, during his confinement; and his family (if any) to be taken care of.

IX. No sort of gaming, or *sky-larking* to be allowed during our meetings, under penalty of sixpence for every offence.

X. Every man is to behave himself with the strictest attention, and walk peaceably in the streets and other places, after Muster; under the penalty of suffering such punishment as the majority shall think fit; as any thing done amiss, will get the whole Body a bad name.

GOD SAVE THE KING.

These the writer believes to be all the private papers that were amongst them, and is sorry to find so many false reports of their meetings being considered dangerous to the country: I ask, was ever seamen known to be enemies to their country? Let every man in England, put the question to himself and find what answer his conscience will give him; have they ever at the conclusion of any war been found to hold illegal assemblies ?—I believe at the end of the former war with *America* they were also in great distress, and assembled together until their complaints were heard and redressed, they then went quietly on board their ships, which I venture to say would have been the case now, had they been offered employment for all ; it was no mercenary views that led them to assemble, they have been told, if they had stood out for seven pounds a voyage they would have got it ; that was not their request, they all wanted a little to keep the miserable spark of life from extinguishing till trade should increase. The proposals held out to them by the Owners were rejected, knowing that very few more than the usual number would be taken, and they had resolved not to accept of any terms but such as would employ them all ; this so grieved the Owners they applied for NAVAL and MILITARY force to protect their *Persons* and *Property* which they pointed out to be in the utmost danger, when in fact the only danger their Property was liable to, was what pleased Divine Providence to send—such as gales of wind and strong tides ; and as to the danger their persons were in, it was only what they pleased to bring upon themselves, by inebriety at their general meetings, it being never the intention of the British Tars to disgrace themselves by laying hands upon either them or their property.—

They certainly had for a plea, that the *well disposed seamen*, were not allowed to go on board their ships, but what were the others out of employ to do? had they gone to *their* doors to beg, it is to be feared they would have turned them away with a stern countenance, exclaiming " Begone you lazy Rascal!" Men driven to such extremities, know not how to act; every scene of his past hardships rushes into his mind, and brings from his manly heart and eyes, those sighs and tears which never before, in the midst of severest trials, found vent. Counting over the many years he has languished in foreign climes, he finds his constitution impaired,—he looks back on the battles he has fought with a Howe, a Nelson, a Collingwood, or a Duncan, and gazing on the scars of many a wound, he counts them all as trifles to this last piece of ingratitude and inhumanity—that of being left to perish with hunger! I am aware there are many who will say those who have been on board of men of war, have pensions: to these I answer, there are thousands who have been there many years, and have not one farthing of provision made for them: those who have been from fourteen to twenty years, have one shilling per day,—will that in these times keep a man in victuals, house-rent, and cloaths, how much worse must he be if he has a family.

I shall pass by many trifling occurrences during the time the Seamen held their meetings, as not being worthy of notice, and proceed to the disgraceful scene of Saturday the 21st, when the Seamen who kept watch on the river for the purpose of keeping the ships in the harbour, were at their dinners. At ebb tide they hauled their boats on shore, when Marines were dispatched from His Majesty's Ships, and without a single man to oppose them, cut and destroyed every boat. The writer firmly believes it was never the determination of the Seamen to oppose any force that might be sent against them, which was clearly proved on the following day ; for when several boats were boarded by the Marines, the crews quietly left them, and these boats were also cut to pieces. [*Query. These boats were all private property, by the destruction of them, many have lost their all,—who pays for them, the King, or the Owners?*]

On Monday the 23d inst. the Owners again resolved that protection was held out to every well disposed Seamen who wished to go on board, but that the whole body of the Seamen should have forty eight hours to consider whether they would accept of the former proposals, that of the ships being inspected by the Committees of the Insurances, and that the ships should not sail until such arrangement was made. This was never waited for ; most of the men of North Shields fled to their ships, others to the ships of South Shields and New-castle, turning the clothes of the men who had formerly belonged to them on shore ; the Owners availing themselves of the moment, (thoughtless of the *Honor* they had held out to the Seamen not to go without, on an average, two extra men in each ship,) put the

ships to sea with the usual insufficient number
of men, leaving after every ship was manned
in the harbour, not less then four thousand of
the best sailors unemployed. It is to be hoped
that speedy relief will be made for those ill-
treated, unfortunate men, otherwise they must
lay themselves and families on the parish,
which will be heaping distress upon distress.

━━━━◦◦◦◦◦◦◦◦◦━━━

Now when the blasts of War are o'er,
  Shall Britain leave her Conquering Sons:
Imploring Bread from door to door,
  Regardless of the deeds they've done,

O blush ye Britons at the thought,
  Mark each pale and languid eye!
Hard for you each Tar has fought,
  Can you leave them thus to die?

Stormy Nights and bitter Days
  Have they felt upon the flood;
Where their fates in varied ways
  Led them on to Scenes of blood.

Battle's heat nor Tempest's roar,
  Ne'er their Courage could subdue.
Frozen Pole, or Burning Shore,
  Found our Seamen ever true.

Scorching Days on Indian Seas,
  Saw our Heroes still the same;
Shuddering 'neath the Northern breeze,
  Adding Laurels to each Name.

Shall pale WANT in death-like Terror,
  Seize upon the fearless brave?
Save them Britons lest to-morrow
  Some may find an early grave.

FINIS.

A

FEW REMARKS

ON

THE STATE OF THE LAWS,

AT PRESENT IN EXISTENCE,

FOR REGULATING

Masters and Work-People,

INTENDED AS

A Guide for the Consideration of the House,

IN THEIR DISCUSSIONS

ON THE BILL FOR REPEALING SEVERAL ACTS RELATING
TO COMBINATIONS OF WORKMEN, AND FOR MORE
EFFECTUALLY PROTECTING TRADE, AND FOR
SETTLING DISPUTES BETWEEN MASTERS
AND SERVANTS.

———

" It is in the power of every one to do a great deal if he will; and
the more he does the more ability and inclination he will find for his
exertions."

———

LONDON:

PRINTED FOR THE AUTHORS,
AND TO BE HAD AT 24, BRIDGE STREET, WESTMINSTER.

——

1823.
Price Five Shillings.

G. SIDNEY, Printer,
Northumberland Street, Strand.

DEDICATION.

PETER MOORE, ESQ.

Sir,

In the name of the labouring and manufacturing classes of the community, on whose behalf we are exerting our humble efforts, to effect some amendment of the present oppressive and unequal Code of Laws, which at present only serve to stifle the energy and spirit of industry of that important, and, it may be said, powerful, part of the population of this Kingdom, we beg to offer you our united thanks, for having adopted our undertaking; and, trusting to the justness of the principles, and the equitable provisions therein laid down, we most respectfully offer the following Observations on the present laws relating to the general regulations between master and man, and confidently leave the subject for the future consideration of the House, and hope that what has been now christened Mr. MOORE's Act, will render any MORE Acts on those heads unnecessary.

We remain,

Sir,

Your very obedient, and

very humble Servants,

THE AUTHORS.

London,
May 17, 1823.

INTRODUCTION.

THE following observations are submitted for the consideration of all persons who may feel themselves in any degree interested in the general welfare of the manufacturing and labouring classes of the community.

It would almost seem to be a libel on the common understanding of Englishmen, to suppose that any body who is possessed of the faculties of thinking and seeing, is void of such considerations, did we not meet, daily and hourly, with instances, in our intercourse with the world, of individuals who, because Providence has placed them beyond the reach of want, at least in obtaining all the superfluities and worldly luxuries of this life, (for purposes which our limited means of judging of its great and unerring designs will not allow us to question the wisdom of,) consider the rest of mankind as slaves, sent into the world to minister to their wants and vices, "for it must be owned, that even in this enlightened age, in every department of society, there are still too many whose views are as narrow, whose ideas are as contracted, and whose prejudices are as rooted as ever.

B

The Bill which has this Session been submitted
to Parliament, and which, should that Parliament
in its wisdom and justice suffer to pass into a law,
is the first attempt to enrol, on the already over-
loaded files of Statutes of this kingdom, a code of
laws for the better protection of trade in general ;
a more equitable adjustment of all disputes and
differences which may hereafter arise between
masters and their work-people ; and for protecting
the latter in the due payment of their wages. And
the foundation of this new code will be raised, it is
hoped, on the ashes of a small but not unimportant
part of the present incongruous, inefficient, and
inapplicable piles of Statutes which have too long
been suffered to disgrace the archives of our two
Houses of Parliament.

There is an old saying, and a very true one, viz.
" What is anybody's business is nobody's ;" but
which we may with equal truth read, (as an Irish-
man would say,) backwards, viz. " what is nobody's business is anybody's." And therefore
it is that this attempt is made to ameliorate the
condition of the labouring classes of the community,
and in so doing, the situation and interest of the
masters will be found to have shared equally in the
considerations which have led to the framing of the
present proposed law.

It will perhaps be said, that as our manufacturing towns are all in such a flourishing condition,
there surely can need no alteration in any of the

laws applicable to those classes, who are so well off. Whether that assertion is founded on the answers which may have been received, to a list of queries, which the public were informed had been sent round through the different manufacturing districts, by the direction of the Right Honourable gentleman who presides at the head of the Home Department, is not known : but all we know is, that if there has been any answers returned, the precise nature of them is not known, although the queries to which those answers were to be made, the public are already in possession of.

In the absence, therefore, of such desirable information, before we enter into the particular object of these observations, it may not be unimportant to the view which we have taken of the several laws which have from time to time, from the earliest ages, been passed, to regulate the manufacturing classes of this Kingdom, to lay before our readers a copy of a letter which the knowledge of our undertaking has produced, from a person in the centre of our manufacturing districts, which will afford a slight specimen, but, it is feared, a very true one, of what may be anticipated as the answer to the list of queries alluded to above. After stating the lively interest which the bare intimation of the attempt to mend the present laws applicable to the manufacturing classes, has created among those districts of Warwick, Derby, and Nottingham, and rejoicing that, for once, good has arose from

evil, (which the continued neglect of His Majesty's
Government, in not directing any portion of their
atttention to such an important object, has hitherto been justly considered,) by inducing others to
lend their assistance in the furtherance of so important an object; he goes on to say;—"I am per-
" fectly aware that Ministers always view with a
" jealous eye every measure which emanates from
"" the left hand of the speaker:" (alluding to the
Honourable member who has kindly fathered the
present undertaking;) " but then the code is in
" such a wretched state that they must interfere.
" There are whole neighbourhoods of thieves in
" manufacturing towns, No laws to protect mas-
" ters in gold, silver, brass, lead, tin, pewter, or any
" other metal but iron. The paper and press work-
" ing masters unprotected from embezzlement; nay,
" in fact, almost all the trades in England are un-
" protected, either as to materials or wages. The
" first workmen in the country emigrating, because
" they can flourish better in France than in Eng-
" land. In fact, without some decisive steps on
" the part of the Legislature, the manufactures
" of Britain are breaking up, and setting towards
" France. We certainly have, for the last thirty
" years, enjoyed the benefit of an immense mono-
" poly of skill, talent, and machinery ; but the next
" ten years will change the scene indeed, unless the
" Bill which you present, or some one similar to it,
" is passed. The clause which gives the holder of

" the machine power to summons for his loss of
" time and expense, is of immense importance to
" the encouragement of inventions by the operative
" workmen. The law is now totally in favour of
" the master, and the end of it is, that the master
" is grinding down the workman, till he looks upon
" work as a secondary employment. The master
" having taught him to become dishonest, he takes
" every advantage of society, and becomes a thief.
" This is the case with us; we can scarcely walk the
" streets, and scarcely a night passes but houses
" are broken into. Penal laws are at an end: the
" thieves are so numerous, they run the hazard of
" the gallows, or transportation; it has lost its effect
" to a very great extent. This I know to be true,—
" labour is so low in a number of branches of ma-
" nufacture in this country, that the young persons
" cannot be brought to labour, as they can steal
" more in one night than they can earn in a week.
" They regard no more a person being hanged of
" their acquaintance, than a soldier does his com-
" rade falling. The convicts, when they leave,
" generally give and receive a huzza! from their
" companions. Such is the number of persons
" transported, that it has ceased to be a disgrace;
" and parents talk of their boy at the hulks, in the
" way of soldiers in the army; and, to speak the
" real and naked truth, we have not now so much
" crying for a child transported, as we used to have
" when he was marched off to join the army. This

" dreadful state of things may last some time, but
" the end must be terrible indeed. If the Minis-
" ters do not know of this state of society, I am
" indeed sorry for them: they will feel it, and my
" poor country also will too soon."

Let any man who has any of the *amor patriæ*
left in him, read the foregoing description, and then
let him blush when he learns such is the situation
of the far greater portion of the most valuable part
of the community of this once great and flourishing
nation.

The late Marquis of Londonderry had a favorite
expression, upon which he seemed at all times, and
upon all occasions, to have as much faith in as
Macbeth had in the weird sisters, viz.—" *Have patience, gentlemen, and trust to the general working
of events.*" And to what a precious head have
those workings fretted themselves, when the present
state of the country could suggest to any man's mind
the description which the writer above has given
of that part of the community which your political
economists, of the present day, now wish the country to consider as the real source of all its greatness.
Alas! what has become of the pride of the Aris-
tocracy, and the once standing toast of former
days, " The Plough ?"—when the only transforma-
tion of which it was ever considered susceptible,
was being converted into a sword for its own defence. Whereas, now it is rent into a thousand
shreds, to form Spinning Jennies, by the power of

whose mechanism it has hurled its former patrons, possessors, and employers, to destruction; and it will require but little more of the same system "*of the general working of events*," to complete the total destruction of the present outward appearances of the prosperity of this country, founded, as they really are, on a total disunion of all the common interests that should bind man and man in one regular gradation of society, but which can only be permanently kept together by such a system of legislation as, while it secures to the rich man the full enjoyment of his wealth, it provides for the poor man a just and equitable price for his labour, and a fair and open field to exercise that labour to the best advantage, which he cannot do to his own benefit without, at the same time, diffusing tenfold advantage to every branch of that society of which he is a member: for, to borrow the words of an Honourable Member of the House,* " Although to the territorial extent of the United Empire nature has set bounds, to the spirit and exertions of its inhabitants I know of none. By extending our improvements in Agriculture and Manufactures to the highest points of which they are capable, the population might be doubled, and the United Empire, enjoying the blessings of a really free constitution, honesty and fairly administered, in all its parts,

---

* Mr. Curwen.

would present so firm and united a Body as might
bid defiance to all the efforts of the Slaves of Despo-
tism;" and, as Falconbridge says " Come the three
corners of the world in arms, and we shall shock
them: nought shall make us rue, if England to itself do rest but true."

A FEW REMARKS

ON THE

PRESENT STATE OF THE LAWS,

&c. &c. &c.

" Who is the real benefactor ? he who relieves present
distress. Give every one what he needs at the present moment.
Do not amuse him with fine words who is starving, but give
him bread. Of what use is a guinea to a drowning man ? fetch
him out of the water."

BEFORE we come to the recital of the various
laws already in existence, applicable to this subject,
it may not be amiss to say a few words upon the
subject of the payment of wages, low as they are,
particularly when a nation is entertained by some of
your theoretical political economists, and, if report
is to be believed, in very high quarters, of relieving
the landed interest by a relaxation of the present
laws regulating the payment of labourers' wages in
money, (particularly as one of the objects of the
present measure is to draw the line more closely,
and, if possible, less easy of evasion than it now
proves to be ;) for it has been imagined, that the allowing the payment of wages in goods would lead to
a greater consumption of agricultural produce, and
thereby create a re-action in the present depressed
state of our corn markets. The bare supposition

of such a result is sufficient, in the present day, to catch the ear of the landed gentlemen; and some excuse may be made for the readiness with which they may have been foolishly deluded with such a will o'the wisp.

In the first place, the only reason which could induce the master manufacturers to seek for such a violation of common justice would be, what is no doubt the case at present, a great scarcity of the circulating medium. But then the merchant must mind, that in case he should succeed so far as to get a repeal of those laws, that he gets a clause introduced into his new bill, to provide that the farmer shall be obliged to take his (the manufacturer's,) goods in exchange for his, (the farmer's,) goods, as it is presumed the payment is to consist of goods the produce of this country; and, if so, I think we need not waste another word to prove the absurdity of such a proposition. Should it, however, be in contemplation of leaving the master manufacturer a choice of the articles he may think best suits his interest, the following circumstances will afford some specimen of what would be the effects of such a system of things, and which, perhaps, has given rise to the proposition for this practice, and will shew at the same time, if left to the option of the manufacturer, what description of goods he is likely to want, and consequently the market he is most likely to go to for them.

" This practice, notwithstanding the existing

laws, which punisheth this offence by the recovery of the wages so paid in goods, and by a penalty of not less than £10, has been openly and daringly carried on by one Lace Manufacturer in this town, for more than 14 years, in the cotton and silk manufactures, to the great annoyance of the respectable lace manufacturers, to the oppression of his poor work-people, and the great injury of the retail tradesmen, who deal in the various articles which this man has palmed on those persons whom he has employed. The example which he has had the temerity to give, has been followed by a great number of other persons, and had it not been for these salutary laws being in some measure enforced during the late unparalleled distress of trade, this practice would have been nearly totally adopted, so that the work-people of this extensive manufacturing district would have been supplied by their masters with their provision, clothing, &c. instead of being paid in money to circulate among the tradespeople who deal in those articles.

"This individual, who has set so pernicious an example to the rest of the lace manufacturers, and masters in the lace and hosiery trades, has been summoned before the magistrates of the town of Nottingham for the recovery of the sum of £81 which he had advanced to one of his workmen in goods instead of money. The magistrates, according to law, ordered the wages to be paid in money, with which this individual refused to

comply; a warrant was issued to levy the money
by distress, when he endeavoured to intimidate
them from doing their duty, by sending them a
notice of action to PROSECUTE THEM for the tres-
pass. Not content with this, he applied to these
Magistrates to suffer him to appeal after he had
neglected to take the steps directed by the law
for that purpose; this was granted to him, on condition of his withdrawing his notice of action, and
agreeing to abide by the decision of the Recorder
and the Bench of Justices in full Sessions. To
this he consented; his appeal was heard; the order of the Magistrates was affirmed, after a long
and patient hearing by the Recorder, Wm. Reader,
Esq. when his Attorney declared, that he was not
satisfied with the exposition of the law given by
the Learned Counsel, but that he should apply to
the Court of King's Bench for a writ of *certiorari*,
to compel the Magistrates to certify what they had
done, that the opinion of the Judges might be taken
thereon. Upon this the Court directed that the
workman's wages should be withheld, until the
issue of the application was known, as great doubt
existed whether the *certiorari* was not taken away
by a recent act of parliament; his Attorney
pledging himself to apply to the King's Bench the
next term, and if he did not obtain the writ the
ensuing term, the money was to be paid to the
workman. The next term, he did not apply to the
Court of King's Bench; and when the workman

applied for his wages according to the order of Sessions, this impudent Lawyer sent the Magistrates and the workman a new notice, that he should apply to the Judges' Chambers for a writ of *certiorari*, as Mr. Clarke had *forgot* to apply for the writ in open term. This application was made, and Mr. Justice Bailey refused the writ. Notwithstanding which the money was still withheld. Application was then made on the part of the workman in open Session for his wages; which application, this "thrice ladle-rubbed" Lawyer, with unblushing front stood to oppose, on the ground that he would have money to resist him in his further law operations. The wages were directed by the Court to be paid, notwithstanding his efforts. In the ensuing term, in February last, he at length applied to the Court of King's Bench, for a writ of *certiorari*, and a *mandamus* to command the Magistrates to hear THE CAUSE OVER AGAIN!!!!!! The Judges declined granting the *certiorari* upon the *exparte* statement of Mr. Scarlett, but granted a rule, requiring the poor law-harassed workman to show cause why a writ of *certiorari* should not be issued. On Monday last, in the Court of King's Bench, Mr. Scarlett moved the Court to make the rule absolute, and to grant a writ of *certiorari*. This was opposed by Mr. Denman, on the part of the workman, but the Judges being of opinion, that the words of the act were not explicit enough to take away the *certiorari*, were under the necessity of granting the writ. Thus compelling the poor workman, after applying for his wages which had been unjustly and unlawfully kept from him on account of goods, which, in many instances, had been charged full double price, on the 1st of May, 1821, to appear in the Court of King's Bench, to defend himself by Counsel, on the 7th of June, 1822; thirteen months after the complaint to the Magistrates, and that too at an expense exceeding the whole amount of the wages he has recovered.

" The object of this litigation is not to recover the wages back again, but to deter other poor work-people from making similar applications to the laws of their country for justice; and by some law chicanery or other, if he can make his motion unopposed, render the provisions of the Act nugatory, and thus be enabled to furnish the persons in his employment with goods instead of money. The consequence of which will be, that the rest of the manufacturers must adopt his practice and the rest of his coadjutors, in paying in goods, or suffer them to take away their business, as no manufacturer who pays in money can, by any possibility, compete with those who pay in goods. The decided object, therefore, of this brace of worthies, the lawyer and his client, who aims at being both manufacturer and tradesman, is to make the law of none avail, that he may be enabled to become a dealer in the following trades, as the list of goods which he has

furnished to two of his work-people will satisfacto-
rily prove; viz. haberdasher, hatter, linen-draper,
woollen-draper, jeweller, watch-maker, umbrella-
maker, laceman, cabinet-maker, ironmonger, butter
and cheesemonger, onion-monger, sack-bag-man,
undertaker, together with which he has FURNISHED
PRETTY LARGELY in the BRANDY AND GIN
LINE! and at the moment when this poor workman applied for his wages, he had furnished some
of his poor work-people with a large quantity of
LEMONS, the greater part of which were damaged;
he being fearful of the operations of the law, these
lemons were destroyed, not being fit for sale to any
other tradesman.

LIST OF ARTICLES

FURNISHED TO THE WORKMAN IN QUESTION.

	£	s.	d.
29lbs. Dutch Butter, at 1s. 5½d. per lb.	£1	17	5½
To sundry goods	1	8	0
14½ yards calico, 1s. 4½d. per yard	0	19	11
3 yards linen, at 2s. 6d. per yard	0	7	6
1 doz. calico fents	0	8	6
7 yds. print, at 2s. 3d. per yd.	0	15	9
Half piece ribbon	0	7	0
4 yds. broad-cloth, at 26s per yd.	5	4	0
2 yds. broad-cloth, at 25s. per yd.	2	10	0
5½ yds. of cord, at 9s. 6d. per yd.	2	13	3
Hat	0	18	6
Umbrella	1	10	0
15 yds. print, at 1s. 8d. per yd.	1	5	0
22 yds. dimity, at 1s. 4d. per yd.	1	9	4
Half yard cambric, at 18s. per yd.	0	9	0

13 silk handkerchiefs, at 7s. 3d. each	£3	12	3
3 scarfs, at 10s. 6d. each	1	11	6
3 yds. lace, at 2s. per yd.	0	6	0
2 yds. lace, at 5s. per yd.	0	10	0
2 yds. blue cloth, at 32s. per yd.	3	4	0
PARASOL	1	0	0
7 silk handkerchiefs, at 7s. 6d. each	2	12	6
2 metal foreign watches	3	15	0
5¾ yds. broad-cloth, at 26s. per yd.	7	9	6
TEA CHEST	1	10	0
25 YARDS OF LINEN, at 4s. 3d. per yd.	5	6	3
TWO BUSHELS DUTCH ONIONS	2	4	0
7 yds. broad-cloth, at 28s. per yd.	9	16	0
4 yds. cord, at 10s. 6d. per yd.	2	2	0
9½ yds. stuff, at 2s. 8d. per yd.	1	5	4
15 yards print, at 2s. 6d. per yd.	1	17	6
10 yds. sprigged cambric, at 2s. 9d. per yd.	1	7	6
Bed quilt	0	3	6
11 yds. muslin, at 2s. 4d. per yd.	1	5	8
2½ yds. broad-cloth, at 27s. per yd.	3	7	6
1 piece of calico	1	1	0
8 yds. cord, at 10s. 6d. per yd.	4	4	0
BROACH	0	10	0
7½ yds. gown piece, at 2s. 4d. per yd.	0	17	6
Scarf	1	8	0
15 sack bags, at 1s. 6d. each	1	2	6
10 yds. black velveteen, AN OLD MOURNING PALL, QUITE ROTTEN, at 1s. 6d. per yd.	0	15	0

PAID TO A POOR MENDER GIRL,
IN HIS WAREHOUSE.

2¼ yds. lace, at 2s. 2d. per yd.	£0	5	5
2 gowns and a scarf	2	1	3
Silk handkerchief	0	7	6
Gown piece	1	5	0

Shawl	0	19	0
7 yds. blue print	0	7	7
Umbrella	0	7	0
2¾ yds. pelisse-cloth, at 14s. 6d. per yd.	1	19	10½
Umbrella	0	8	0
3 yds. ribbon	0	2	0
FIRE IRONS	0	9	0
2 tea trays	0	17	0
Lace cap	0	8	6
10 yds. stuff, at 1s. 6d. per yd.	0	15	0
5½ yds. stuff, at 2s. 6d. per yd.	0	13	9
6 yds. stuff, at 2s. 3d. per yd.	0	13	6
5½ yds. blue stuff, at 3s. 3d. per yd.	0	17	10¼
7 yds. blue stuff, at 1s. 8d. per yd.	0	11	8
4½ lbs. salt Dutch butter, 1s. 4d. per lb	0	6	0
Half peck Dutch onions	0	2	6*

* Since writing the above the case has been decided in the
Court of King's Bench.

COURT OF KING'S BENCH,

Wednesday, April 30, 1823.

The King v. Thomas Kayes.—This was a conviction of Mr.
Kaye, a master lace manufacturer, under 12 Geo. I., cap. 34,
for paying a workman in goods instead of money, in contra-
vention of that act which was passed to protect workmen from
the evil of being compelled by their masters to take part of
their wages in goods. In this case the master originally contracted with the workmen to pay in goods ; and the question
was, whether the statute prohibited such a contract, or only
inflicted a penalty on the master who, having agreed generally
with his servant for wages, paid him afterwards otherwise than
in money. Mr. Solicitor General, Mr. Common Sergeant, and
Mr. Tindal agreed that the statute prohibited all payment
except by money, even when such satisfaction was given in
pursuance of a previous contract. Mr. Scarlett, and Mr. Lit

C

After reading the specimen above, it is presumed little more will be required to convince the farmer that such a system could afford him very little relief ; and as a proof of how little it would benefit the Chancellor of the Exchequer, in enhancing the revenue, the following few necessary accompanyments to such a system will, it is presumed, be equally convincing of its impracticability, to say nothing of its injustice.

Acts which must be repealed in order to render the payment of Labourer's wages in goods, legal payment, or even to render it practicable, if it can be seriously thought of for a moment.

First. The 4th Edw. 4th, cap. 1st, as to woollen cloth manufacturers.

---

tledale contended, on the other side, that such construction would be absurd, unjust, and in manifest restraint of commerce. The court suggested that there was a technical error in the conviction which was fatal, inasmuch as the words of the statute were not pursued. They, therefore, quashed the proceedings without giving any opinion as to the main point raised for their decision. After the judgment had been given,

The Lord Chief Justice remarked, that the acts on the important subjects of masters and workmen were extremely difficult to construe, from the uncertain wording and the complexity of their provisions. As he observed three gentlemen engaged in this case who had seats in parliament, he hoped he might effectually draw their attention to the state of a law so important to the public interests. He thought it right to point out the evil, but he would not presume to suggest the remedy.

Second. The 8th Eliz. cap. 13, as to Shrewsbury.

Third. The 1st of Anne, Stat. 2d. cap. 18, as to woollen, linen, cotton, and leather manufactures.

Fourth. The 10th Anne, Do. Do. &c.

Fifth. 12th Geo. 1st. cap. 34, Do. Do. as to woollen, &c.

Sixth. 22d Geo. 2d. cap. 27, as to woollen, cotton, &c.

Seventh. 29th Geo. 2d. cap. 33, as to woollen manufacture.

Eighth.

Ninth. 57th Geo. 3d. cap. 115, as to steel and plated goods.

Tenth. 57th Geo. 3d. cap. 122, as to colliers.

Eleventh. 58th Geo. 3d. cap. 51, as to cash payments, and altering distribution of penalties.

Three coal-heavers' Acts.

Acts respecting summons for wages.

First 20th Geo. 2d. cap. 19.

All Acts for the recovery of small debts, as well as the present powers of Courts of Requests, or County Courts, should provide that no master, on tender of amount of wages in goods, shall be held to bail. Vide 58th Geo. 3d. legal tender in paper money.

53d Geo. 3d. cap. 114, as to the issuing of local tokens, as masters will pay in pieces of copper, though unstamped, which copper tokens will pass current in districts.

To amend hawkers' and pedlars' Act; to allow workmen or their families, or agents, to hawk and sell goods received as wages, without license.

To amend Auction duty Act, and suffer such goods to be sold duty free.

To amend Pawnbrokers' Act, as to the rate of interest.

To provide for distress of rates, and king's taxes, to be paid for in goods, at the rate at which the person receives them; or compel master to make good the loss by sale. The same as to payment of rent, poor, and church rates, paving rates, and all other outgoings in the shape of rates and taxes.

To amend existing laws as to short weights and measures, which at present only extend to selling. Also as to adulterating flour, which now likewise only relates to sellers.

Also the present law respecting butchers' meat not fit for food.

Also the present excise laws, prohibiting the making or selling of less quantity than

Also respecting licenses to publicans and spirit merchants, as masters may pay in ale and spirits, though servants may not sell.

From the time of the 23d Edw. 3d, up to the 53rd Geo. 3rd, the magistrates had power to fix the rate of wages, which must be paid in money.

This was the invariable course pursued till the Revolution. In the reign of James 1st, and Charles 1st, commissioners were appointed to enforce those laws, and a number of Star Chamber decrees were made, from the reign of Henry 7th, to the abolishing of that court, in the reign of Charles the 1st, enforcing the fixing the rate of wages, and fining magistrates for neglect of duty in that respect. The preamble of the Act of Henry 7th, establishing the Star Chamber, states, for the better putting the laws in force, which had been neglected by the magistrates, consequently payment otherwise than in money was illegal, and impracticable, even in those days ; since which two acts have been passed, fixing the rates of tailors' wages and providing that the same shall be paid in money ; one as late as the beginning of the last reign. The last Acts for fixing the rate of wages, are the Spitalfields Acts, 1st, 13th Geo. 3rd cap. 68. 2nd, 32nd Geo. 3rd, cap. 44th, and 43rd Geo. 3rd Cap. 151, whereby the Justices fix the rate of wages in money. These, though local Acts, must be repealed, to put all other manufacturing districts upon an equal footing.

And which last recited Acts have lately been made the subject of much discussion, in two pamphlets, one an anonymous one, entitled " Observations on the ruinous tendency of the Spitalfields Act." The other, entitled " The good and bad Effects of high and low Wages ; or, a Defence of the Spitalfields Act," in answer to the first, by Andrew Larcher, who, after very ably refuting the whole of the anonymous pamphlet, concludes with the following sentence.

" To conclude, I remind my candid readers, that I have not pretended to be exact in any of my calculations ; have only stated probable conjectures. In respect to the number of working families, I have supposed two millions, and their average wages to be twenty shillings a week to each : but in London they certainly have greater sums than in other parts of the kingdom, where house-rents and all other things are much cheaper. Now, admitting that my conjectures are correct, then there are only £2,000,000, that properly circulate in the ordinary course of trade, for any real benefits to the people. As for the many thousands, tens and hundreds of thousands pounds that go from one to another among " the most opulent" at the stock exchange, the buying and selling of large estates, law suits or litigations, and the sums exchanged for diamonds and other spangled and costly things, (of little more use than tinselled toys) is only taken out of one and locked up in another rich coffer ; but for the purposes of war, the money is drawn forth by many millions for loans to government ; then indeed it gives great increase to trade and employ in all things requisite for war. But, all such loans being added to the national debt, the people are then hampered with more taxation to pay the interest thereof. Now if so many millions can be brought from the stagnant hoards for the purposes of war, then I enquire for a reason why the sum of two millions cannot be added to wages to remove or alleviate all the calamities of the nation, which were brought on by the late wars, especially when it is evident that all such money so added to wages will so greatly increase trade and employ, and return weekly to tradesmen with increased advantage, by a double sale of goods, and to the most opulent, through the numerous channels of taxation, by a double consumption of taxed articles ; as natural, as constant and sure as the waters which flow from the sea return again. But, such benefits cannot be produced but by sufficient wages ; for certainly as may be the condition of working families, so in proportion must be the condition of all other families, from the most wealthy merchants and wholesale tradesmen, down to the lowest retailing shopmen. I defy a refutation of this asser· tion. For if only one person cannot buy, tradesmen must sell less; but when millions of people cannot buy, thousands of tradesmen must fail. And such is now the general failure and distress that pervades the whole kingdom, and causes the word *reformation* to resound through all parts of England, and fills with alarming terrific fears all people who live in ease and affluence, lest reformation should turn to revolution, and bury all their opulence, comforts, and advantages, in that unfathomable

gulf. But sufficient wages will produce all the reformation that is needful to restore plenty, friend-
ship, unity, and loyalty. With a sincere though
hopeless wish that such may be the happy state of
this and of all nations, I conclude."

Having entered into a somewhat more lengthened
exposition of this part of the case than was first
intended, we now proceed to throw into as small a
compass as the nature of the subject will admit of,
a brief account of the different Acts which have
from time to time been passed, from the earliest
times down to the present reign, in order to assist
those to whom it more immediately belongs to frame
the laws of this country, as well as to administer
them, to form a comprehensive view of the whole
subject, regarding masters and servants, and the
grounds upon which the present Bill is framed,
being sensible that the numerous avocations of
members of parliament, frequently prevent them
from paying a strict and minute attention to any
one subject, and consequently they rely on the
works of others who frequently instead of being
practical men, are merely book-worms who write
their own vague imaginations, and consequently
frequently mislead their unwary readers. The
making good and salutary laws for the regulating
of masters and servants is one of the greatest magnitude, as by these laws a national character
and resources are necessarily formed, as all real
property and value of every article arises from

the labour or skill bestowed upon it, *and the spirit and patriotism of the inhabitants of a country will be in proportion to the liberty and means of subsistence which the master and servant enjoys.* But which is, if possible, more forcibly described by the following passage from the pen of a labouring operative mechanic.

" Labour is of all things the most valuable: by " labour all things are produced; but for it the " earth would become a dreary wilderness; and " if the rich live to eat, the poor must eat to live. " The poor man wants not charity, but justice. " Your sympathizing spirit has excited the grate- " ful admiration of a numerous class of smiths, " who hail you as their Day-star, that shall soon " chase away those dense clouds of avarice and " oppression, that the industrious classes of the " community have so long laboured under."

It will be necessary in discussing the provisions of the intended Bill, to review what has been the situation of servants in general, in civilized states, both ancient and modern. The prospect is certainly dreary, and the philanthropic mind is but little cheered by any traces of humanity in the various codes made by legislators for the governing servants and masters,

From the earliest accounts, it appears that the servants of Abraham and his cotemporaries were considered in some measure the property of the master; and it is very evident that the working class in Egypt were in some state of personal thraldom. In Babylon and Nineveh personal slavery seems very generally to have existed, and the Jewish laws certainly tolerate it, though to a very limited extent, but expressly forbid the cruel practice of the early Greeks—man stealing. The Jewish law recognises in the strongest terms the due payment of wages, and directs them to be paid every day, which shews the extreme poverty of servants in those days. The Greeks certainly carried this to a very great extent, and Lycurgus in particular seems to consider the Helots as an inferior grade of beings. Even Solon tolerates slavery, and punishes the crimes of slaves in a very severe manner. The divine Plato, as he has been called, though a man of considerable humanity, seems to have considered the slaves as a distinct race of beings, and requires them to be punished in a cruel manner if they resist or strike their master or owner. The Romans, it appears, were not much behind the Greeks in their notions of slavery, but then they had the wisdom to make sumptuary laws for their regulation and support; but, notwithstanding all this, there is not the least doubt that the revolt of the slaves, and their running away to Germany, &c., was one of the great leading causes which brought about the destruction of that empire. It cannot be denied that the progress of Christianity in some measure paved the way for the abolition of personal slavery. The barbarians of the north, though they abolished slavery as far as regarded themselves, yet they in a great measure kept up many of its evil and unjust practices, by keeping the conquered population in a state of vassalage and dependence on themselves. That the Britons and Saxons sold their children into slavery there cannot be the least doubt, and, that during the time of the Saxon monarchs slavery existed is notorious, as by the laws of Ina and Alfred freemen and villans are distinctly named. I am well aware that from the privileges which were granted by Athelstan and Edward, which are yet extant to certain great towns, as Beverley, &c., that the term may mean no more than that the inhabitant of a large town incorporated with privileges to chuse their own magistrates, and govern their own affairs, might, in the language of the day, be termed freemen, and the villagers, without those privileges, villans. This idea is certainly confirmed by Magna Charta, and by 9 Henry III., cap. 14, which says expressly, that a villan (not the king's) may be amerced if he fall into the king's mercy, saving his wainage. By doomsday's book, it appears that the king's manors amounted to 1024, consequently, in those days the king's villans must amount to a great number of persons, and Magna Charta, which confirmed the right of the crown to fine the Lords' villans, yet restrained the fine to the wainage, that is, to the implements of husbandry, &c. It therefore appears

that the villans were not altogether servants, but
farmers; this is very obvious from the statute of
homage, 17 Edward II., stat. 2, which has a similar form for a freeman and a villan, and appears
to differ little in form, save and except that the
villan promises to hold his land in body and goods,
and the freeman to perform his services. By the
statute of Marlborough, 52 Henry III., cap. 3, the
lords of manors are prevented from distressing freemen for services not due, and by 52 Henry III.,
chap. 22, lords of manors are prevented from compelling freeholders or freemen from answering to
their freeholders without the king's writ; that is,
that he shall not turn him out of his farm without
leave of the king; and by the 28 Edward I., cap.
14, it is declared that farms shall not be let too
dear; therefore it is evident that the freeholder was
a servant as well as the villan, but the law certainly protected him from imposition more than the
villan. By the statute of Frankpledge, 18 Edward
II, (1325) the jurors are directed to enquire if
there be any of the king's villans fugitive, and
dwelling otherwhere than in the king's demesnes
more than a year and a day, and also to enquire
concerning any lord's villans; by this it appears
that either the servants were a distinct body, or
that every peasant had land, and that his services
to his lord were rated, and that not "too dear."
This relates only to husbandry, for in the cities it
is well known that they, the freemen or inhabitants,

governed themselves, and a residence of a twelve
month and a day made a freeman. This is evident from 1 Edward III., stat. 2, cap. 9, which
declares that cities, boroughs, and franchised towns
shall enjoy their usages and customs; and by 9
Richard II., cap. 2, they are allowed to demand
their villans and neiffs* in great towns. But it is
not until the year 1349 that labourers or servants
are mentioned. 23 Edward III., cap. 1, 2, 3, 4,
5, enacts that every person under the age of sixty
years shall be bound to serve any person that doth
require him, or be imprisoned till he find surety.
Workmen or servants leaving service before time
expired, imprisoned. The old wages and no more
to be given servants. If the lord of a town or
manor offend against this law, to be fined treble the
amount of wages. By the 6th chapter, all dealers
in provisions are bound to sell at reasonable rates,
or forfeit double to the party injured. Mayors
neglecting to rate the price of provisions, to be
fined treble the amount to the parties injured, and
fined by the judges. The preamble to this extraordinary act, the provisions of which were fully in
force till 1389, says, that servants, on account of the
decrease in population, arising from the pestilence,
had demanded treble wages. Two years after, (25
Edw. III., cap. 1,) this act is in the most formal manner re-enacted, and the preamble says, at the prayer
of the commonalty, and fixes the wages of servants in

---

* Quere, Were not neiffs servants to the villans and freemen.

husbandry, the prices of threshing, and declares servants shall live in summer where they lived in winter, and by the 5th chapter, artificers are sworn to use their crafts, as in the 20 Edward III.; that is, compelled to make oath that they will not take higher wages than they did in 1346; to which is added, that servants fleeing out of one shire into another, to be imprisoned. It is evident that this, or a similar restriction, had existed from the days of Alfred, as his dividing the country into counties, hundreds, and tithings, had a restrictive view to prevent persons from wandering, and was the origin of frankpledge. 31 Edward III., cap. 2, the lords of franchises are directed to have the fines of labourers who shall offend against 25 Edward III. By the 34 Edward III., cap. 9, the lords of towns may imprison servants fifteen days if they will not justify themselves, or take work at the rate, or prove they have received only the rate, and the wages of masons and carpenters are fixed. By chap. 10, it appears that the servants still refused to work at the rate of wages fixed by 25 Edward III., and absconded and left their service; it was then enacted, that persons fleeing into other shires should be branded in the forehead with the letter F. The 43 Edward III., cap. 6, again confirms the 25 Edward III. In the next reign, notwithstanding Wat Tyler's riots, this code was still persevered in by 12 Richard II., cap. 5; it is enacted that no servant shall depart from *one hundred to another*, without a testimonial *under the*

king's seal, a servant found wandering without
testimonial, put in the stocks, and inflicts penalties
for giving or taking more than the rates; the 6th
section disarms all servants in husbandry. In the
next year, 13 Richard II., cap. 8, this statute of
25 Edward III. was modified, and the justices had
power to fix the rate of wages by proclamation,
(with victuals or without) of MASONS, carpenters,
TILERS, or other craftsmen or labourers, and shall
also have power to rate the gains of victuallers.
The next reign still maintained the code, and the
4 Henry IV., cap. 14, enacts, that labourers shall
not be hired by the week. But the most extraordinary enactment is 7 Henry IV., cap. 17, which
says, that no man shall apprentice his son or
daughter unless he have, or rent, land to the
amount of twenty shillings ; it therefore appears
that fathers, in order to evade the statutes of
wages, apprenticed their children on advantageous
terms. The conqueror, Henry V., began very
early with the labourers, as by 2 Henry V., cap.
4, it is enacted, that the sheriffs may pursue servants into other counties the same as felons; justices to examine servants and their masters on oath,
and convict them on their own confession, without
taking an inquest. And by 4 Henry V., cap. 4,
the masters contrived to get themselves out of the
scrape, as the penalty for receiving or taking ex-
cessive wages is enacted shall apply to the takers
only.

Having finished the short reign of Henry the Fifth, we have found a great number of parliaments, each endeavouring to keep down the rate of wages by severe enactments, we now come to the reign of Henry the Sixth, or rather to that of his uncles', Gloster and Bedford, and we now arrive at a singular æra ; that is, we find an act of parliament, making it felony to call a meeting of masons, who it seems had entered into a confederacy to evade, or set aside, the 13 Richard II., cap. 8.

It is not a little curious, that this celebrated association, which reckons amongst its members, kings, princes, nobles, and gentlemen, should have been originally framed by a number of poor workmen, for the purpose of keeping up their wages, and that their tilers to guard the door, were really the tilers who had joined the confederacy, that the masters, &c., were really masters who had confederated with the men, that their oaths of secrecy and threatening of death by the hand of the first brother, who divulged their secret, became necessary to protect them from the dreadful law which punished them with death if discovered. That all the farrago of apprentices, accepted masons, tilers, &c., were only gradations invented to keep the main secret to a few to avoid detection, and that all the tales of Hiram and Solomon's temple, of Adam and Noah being masons, of its having existed as a society among the Egyptians, that according to the notions of Thomas Paine, they derived their origin from the druids, all vanishes before two plain acts of parliament. It is not the less singular, and may serve as a moral to mark the incertitude and vicissitude of human events, that the king of England is now, by an existing statute, and several of his brothers are also, liable to be tried for their lives for having caused chapiters and congregations of masons to be assembled. Poor fellows! they little thought, when they met under the terrors of the law, that a few centuries would so alter the state of their society, that it would be thought an honor to belong to it.

Three years after, the parliament still further enforced the 13 Richard II., cap. 8, by the 6 Henry VI., cap. 3, which directed the justices to make proclamation of the wages of every artificer and workman. Two years afterwards it was again confirmed by 8 Henry VI., cap. 8. By the 23 Henry VI. cap. 13, servants in husbandry were compelled to give half a year's notice, and their wages were fixed by proclamation. The 25 Henry VI., constrains the king's villans, in North Wales, to their usual labour.

This system of forcing low wages continued to the year 1463, that is, 114 years. It is not to be supposed that the wages were very low originally, as the Lord Chancellor Fortesque, in the reign of Henry VI., gives a very flattering, but certainly high-coloured, picture of the situation of the labouring

D

classes in his day; but other accounts of the state
of the poor, in the reign of Henry VII., by no
means coincide with it. We now come to the
conclusion of the civil wars between Henry VI. and
Edward IV., and the statute book then contains a
number of prohibitory laws; the 33 Henry VI.
cap. 5, and 3 and 4 Edward IV., cap. 3, pro-
hibit the importation of wrought silks—but the
3 and 4 Edward IV., cap. 4, enacts upon the
" piteous complaint of the artificers of manual oc-
cupations, who are unemployed by the introduction
of foreign deceitful wares," that no person shall import a number of articles in the woollen, silk, lace,
gold, iron, leather, tin, brass, bone, paper, brushes,
wire manufactures, amounting to seventy-six enume-
rations, and the parliament, which next met, directed
that the wages of the woollen cloth makers should
not be paid in goods; this was by 4 Edward IV.,
cap. 1.

The usurper Richard III, took up the question
of his subjects being out of employment, notwithstanding the forced wages. And by the 1 Richard
III., cap. 9, bitter complaint is made of merchant
strangers of Italy, Apulia, and Catalans, residing
in London, and monopolizing goods and wares,
and that great numbers of strangers, artificers,
daily repair to London, &c. and will not work at
hard labour, such as plough or cart, and bring goods
from sea and sell them at fairs, and will not take
any of the king's subjects to work with them, and

after having got rich, leave the kingdom; this statute (which was very popular even in the days of Cromwell, as appears from a petition of the framework knitters of London to the Protector) provides that no foreigner shall take apprentices, or become masters, but shall be servants to the English, and prohibits a greater number of articles than the 3 and 4 Edward IV. cap. 4. We shall proceed, now, a little further on this subject, to shew that the notions held respecting the low price of labour producing distress in a country is not theory, but has occurred in England de facto, and the proof is acts of parliament and star chamber decrees repeatedly reiterated and enacted. After the fall of Richard, the new monarch, by the 1 Henry VII., cap. 9 and 10, re-enacts, 3 and 4 Edward IV. cap. 3, and 1 Richard III., cap. 9, but directs the penalties to himself ; it will be perceived by 3 Henry VII., stat. 2, cap. 1, that the odious star chamber was instituted to give vigour to the executive government, as the justices of the peace, as in modern times, refused to do their duty. 4 Henry VII., cap. 12, again confirms this charge ; by the 11 Henry VII., cap. 22, ¡the wages of servants and handicraftmen are again fixed by statute, but in the next year some glimpse of light seems to have struck their benighted minds, as by the 12 Henry VII., cap. 3, the 11 Henry VII. cap. 22, is repealed, as touching artificers' wages. Henry the Eighth, in his sixth year, again fixed the wages of servants, by the 6 Henry VIII., chap. 3.

But the next year 7 Henry VIII., cap. 5, this was repealed as to labourers or servants.

The principle of 1 Richard III., cap. 9, respecting foreigners taking apprentices, &c. was re-enacted by 14 and 15 Henry VIII , cap. 2 ; this was again confirmed by 21 Henry VIII., cap. 16. In the same year, that is (1428) the celebrated star chamber decree was issued against foreigners, in which it is stated that the cordwainers are put out of employment by aliens, and gives a most deplorable description of the state of the country from thieves, " who were executed in great numbers ;" this decree forbids them from having more than two servants foreigners ; foreigners are allowed to take as many apprentices, being *English householders*, as they can get, and compels them to pay to the cordwainers the same as other crafts. This decree was extremely popular, and the shoemakers, from that time, have regularly kept the holiday of St. Crispin to commemorate it. Cardinal Wolsey was extremely popular in forwarding this decree. The death of Henry the Eighth placed his son upon the throne, who was a minor, therefore his uncle Somerset was the actual ruler, who began in a violent manner to work, to reform the morals of the country by force ; in the 2 and 3 Edward VI., the first general combination act was passed, which extended as well to workmen as dealers in victuals. This act imposeth very heavy fines, for the third offence forty pounds, or else shall *sit* on the pillory, lose one of his ears, and be taken as a man infamous, and his sayings, or oath, not to be taken as evidence. Forty pound was an immense sum in those days, and few persons in the realm was capable of paying forty pounds ; if any company or corporation made any such covenant, such corporation to be disfranchised ; a terrible punishment considered in those days, as they could not carry on their craft when the corporation was disfranchised. The country was so overrun and annoyed with beggars and strolling persons that, by the 1 Edward VI., cap. 3, it was enacted, that if any person should bring before any justice any runagate servant, or other person living idle or disorderly for *three days*, the said justice shall cause him to be marked on the breast, with a hot iron, with the letter V, and adjudge him to be a slave to the person who brought him for two years, who shall feed him on bread and water, and refuse meat ; and cause him to work by beating and chaining, " let the work be never so vile." If such slave shall be absent for fourteen days during the two years, to be marked on the ball of the cheek with the letter S, and shall be adjudged to be a *slave for ever.* If he run away a second time he shall be considered as a felon. For the honour of human nature this act only lasted three years ; the 1 and 2 Philip and Mary, cap. 4, enacts that any gypsies remaining in England one month shall be guilty of felony.

The 3 and 4 Philip and Mary, cap. 3 and 11, shews more the actual state of England during the reign of the Tudors than any other document we ever saw. It appears that not only was the manufactural interest in a wretched condition, but that the agricultural was also. The chap. 11, even interferes as to how many looms a master shall have in his possession, and states, expressly, that the wages in woollen weaving had become so low that numbers had been compelled to leave the employment. The 5 Elizabeth, cap. 3, enacts that land having been kept to tillage for four years, shall be kept to tillage under a penalty of ten shillings, per acre. Having now arrived at the golden days of good Queen Bess, it may not be amiss to take a review of the whole system of legislation, from the 23 Edward III., 1346 to the 5 Elizabeth, 1563, a period of 217 years, during the whole of which the legislature was endeavouring, with a high hand, to keep down the rate of wages; under the erroneous impression that the more the labourer obtained for his work the less there remained for the landholder and the capitalist.

In justice, however, it must be admitted that however cruel, severe, and unjust they were in principle, yet the same parliament extended the same restrictive laws to themselves and to the dealers in provisions, and, in fact, to every thing. By the 3 Edward III., in the parliament held at Nottingham, a statute was passed similar to the sumptuary laws of the Romans, by which a rate was fixed of the number of dishes to be served up at each baron's, &c. table, and the value of them, *this is law now.* The law respecting rents has been already mentioned. The prices of butchers' meat was fixed at a farthing per pound, for nine years, in the reign of Henry VIII. The laws respecting monopolizers, forestallers, and regrators, were equally enforced. Laws to prevent monopoly of farms and sheep; and in order to force the industry of the country, numerous acts were passed to compel persons of every degree to wear certain dresses. This was the law from 1363, 37 Edward III. cap. 8, until the reign of James the First, more than 230 years ; all was in vain, low wages kept the state low ; should it be thought necessary it would be easy to furnish a list of all these restrictive laws. It will, no doubt, be perceived the grand problem of political economy is, that where either the state, the church, the landlord, the master, or any other means, takes from the labourer the greater part of his wages, as soon as it is earned, prevents him from circulating such wages to employ another labourer, and, consequently, the employment instead of increasing through the means of exchange of labour is derived from the unproductive person alone; thus there will be found in all poor states a number of persons unemployed, because the population cannot employ each other, arising from the money being consumed before it has obtained due circulation.

It will be necessary before proceeding to the laws made during the long reign of Elizabeth, in some measure to review the laws made by the Plantagenets and Tudors, to force a trade or the

employment of their population By the 11th
Edw. 3rd, cap. 1, it is made felony to export wool.
Cap. 2, it is enacted that no person shall wear
cloth not made in England. Cap. 3, foreign merchants shall not import cloth under pain of for-
feiture of cloth and imprisonment; and by the 5th
chapter, passed at the same time, which was regarded, (and has been since regarded) as the *mas-
ter-piece* of Edward's policy, "It is accorded that
all cloth-workers of foreign lands, of whatsoever
country they be, who will come into England, Ireland, Wales, or Scotland, within the King's power,
shall come safely and surely, and shall be in the
King's protection and safe conduct, to dwell where
they will. And to the intent the said cloth workers
shall have the greater will to come, the King will
grant them franchises, as many and such as may
suffice them." This certainly drew a number of
cloth workers to Sudbury, South Wales, and other
parts, and laid the foundation for the woollen manufactures of this kingdom. It may be necessary here
to observe, that cloth-working was carried on to a
great extent in this Kingdom, previous to this, and
that Guilds and Fraternities were incorporated in
London, Nottingham, Norwich, and Northampton,
long before this period. These Guilds, now called
Companies, formed a very important part of ancient legislation in England, very little of whose
powers now remain. From an immense number
of laws it appears that it was the intention of the
British legislation to manufacture, by dint of law,

the best and cheapest goods in Europe, as by the
25th Edw. 1, cap. 7th, that monarch released a tax
of no less than 40s. a sack on wool, and that at
a time when wheat was sold for 3s. per quarter.
The intent of the ancient trade companies, it appears, was to prevent false goods being made, and
to encourage the education of skilful workmen ; as
by ancient law, a person must serve seven years
apprenticeship, or he could not work at any trade
or craft ; but at the same time the utmost vigi-
lance was used to prevent them becoming monopolies, which is contrary to the general received
opinion, as is evident from Magna Charta allowing foreigners to trade in large corporated towns ;
and by 2 Rich. 2nd, cap. 1, all charters to that
effect are repealed; and if impediments are made, the
franchise is taken away from the city, and they pay
double damages. Commissioners to enquire into
the premises, were also appointed. In order to encourage a foreign trade, staples were appointed for
the transaction of business ; a mayor and two constables were chosen by the merchants, one denizen
the other alien, well versed in the merchant law,
who were to govern according to *merchant law*, and
punish their own felons and offenders. This was
by 27 Edw. 3rd. These staple laws were again
enacted by 14th Rich. 2nd, cap. 1, and, least they
should be injurious to the English trade, by the same
statute it is enacted that merchant strangers coming
to England with merchandize, shall find sureties to

lay out half the money they take in English goods.
Respecting the jealousy of Parliaments as to the
guilds, 15th Hen. 6th, cap. 6, which restrains
them from making unlawful orders. 7th Edw. 4th
cap. 1, gives authority to the mayor and justices of
Norwich to inquire into the conduct of the wardens
of Norwich. The 3rd Hen. 7th, cap. 9th, punishes
the mayor and aldermen of London for restraining
their freemen. 19th Hen. 7th, cap. 17th, repeals
the 11th Hen. 7th, cap. 11th, and destroys the
power of the wardens of Norwich, because they
had attempted a monopoly and made fines. The
22nd Hen. 8th, cap. 4, inflicts a penalty of £40
on all corporations and fellowships, charging more
than a certain rate for registering apprentices: this
is re-enacted by 26th Henry 8th, cap. 10.

But the most extraordinary restrictions, in order
to produce cheap goods, are the laws which prevent the interest of money. The 15th Edw. 3rd,
cap. 5th, declares that usury should be punished by
the church; and by a proclamation, dated 1st Oc-
tober, 1341, at Westminster, the King declares, that
he was compelled thereto by the Commons, who
refused to proceed to any other business, unless he
would assent; but directs the sheriff to make proclamation, that the statute should be void. 25th
Edw. 3rd, cap. 12, says, that no person shall take
profit for exchange of money. By the 3rd Henry
7th, cap. 6, all chevisance and usury shall be extir-
pated, all brokers of such bargains to be pilloried,

to be imprisoned six months, and fined £20; that is, the interest of money was totally abolished to compel persons to employ their money in trade, and instead of a second person working the money and paying a per centage to the first, the owner was obliged to work his own money. Eight years after, that is by 11th Hen. 7th, cap. 8, usurers was to forfeit one half the sum bargained for.

It may easily be perceived, therefore, that our ancestors tried every scheme that the mind of man almost could invent to employ their population, and accumulate wealth under the restrictive system of low wages; they even went so far as to levy heavy fines on every person not having a sunday dress, as directed by law; but it was utterly useless, as the poor could not purchase clothing; all was due for victuals, even the King's servants were without shoes and stockings, and there is an ordinance extant, forbidding them to sleep before the fire on the hearth;—it is therefore evident, that too low wages is the bane of prosperity of a commonwealth, from actual experience; and, in fact, reason says the same, for in truth the riches of a country consists in the produce of its labour, and if the impetus of labour is removed, which consists in the supplying each the wants of the other, the consequence is, that such a state naturally becomes poor: a population may be partially employed by administering only to the wants or luxuries of *unproductive persons;* but to be wholly employed, to be rich, to be wealthy, to have a large surplus means, the whole population must be employed, and that too to the advantage of each other. A very large amount of labour may be taken from such a population, which will be little felt; but take the same amount from a population which labour merely to supply the first wants of nature, and for unproductive persons, and the greatest distress immediately occurs. In fact, it can only be continued for a short time ; witness European and Asiatic states compared with Britain and France.

Elizabeth, as soon as she was firmly seated on the throne, after the defeat of the armada, set about, in some measure, ameliorating the condition of the servants and artificers in England ; and though the code was still arbitrary, yet, at the same time, some of its harshest provisions were repealed : it is not a little singular, that for a period of 260 years, from 1563 to 1823, no member should propose to carry into effect a bill to consolidate the laws respecting masters and servants, from the time of Elizabeth till we have now taken it up. The 5 Elizabeth, cap. 4, does what we are now attempting to do, repeals all the laws respecting the hiring, keeping, departing, working, wages, or orders of servants, workmen, artificers, &c.

The situation of Elizabeth was critical, but yet she had great power and resources unknown to any of her predecessors since the time of the conqueror. Her grandfather, Henry VII. had put the finishing stroke to the power of the barons, by abolishing their

retainers; for though various attempts had been
made for this purpose by Edward III. and Henry
IV., yet it was not till the reign of Henry VII.
that these petty monarchs were forbidden to keep
troops in their pay. But the power and consequence of the crown was immediately restored by
the acts of resumption of the crown lands, by the
1 Henry VII., 3 Henry VII., 11 Henry VII.
These resumptions had continually taken place in
former reigns, and, by an act passed by Edward II.
it was made felony to receive grants of crown
lands: it is a very singular feature in the statutes
at large, that these acts of resumption of crown
lands are carefully omitted :—by whose orders this
was done it is impossible to say, but as they form a
grand contrast from the revenues of the states in
former times, to the borrowing scheme now adopted,
we subjoin a short list of them :—William I., in the
right of Edward, the Saxon, succeeded to the right
of 1422 manors as terre regis, or crown lands, the
income of which in those days amounted to £1061
10s. 1½d.; and the knights who paid escuage,
amounted to 60,000; this was an immense sum, and
quite commensurate to the expenses of the government without taxation. William Rufus was compelled by the people to resume his own grants;
Henry I. resumed the crown lands which had been
alienated by Ranulphus, Bishop of Durham; Henry
II., when count of Anjou, compelled Stephen to resume his grants; Henry II. resumed his crown lands,

and punished the Earl of Albemarle, who resisted him; Richard I. alienated the crown lands for the crusade, but resumed them on his return; John alienated the whole of his crown lands to Peter de Savoy, and other foreigners, but the barons banished them and caused a resumption; Edward II. gave the crown lands in such abundance to Piers Gaveston, that the barons caused a commission to be made out for their resumption. By the 5 Edward II. the crown lands were resumed, but was revoked by 15 Edward II.; after the defeat and death of the Earl of Lancaster, Edward III. resumed the crown lands after the fall of Mortimer by his own prerogative. The crown lands were alienated by Richard I. in favour of R. de la Poole, Earl of Suffolk, and others, in such profusion, that the parliament of 10, 11, 13 Richard II. restrained him from making grants. 21 Richard II. repeals all these restrictions, and soon after that that monarch ceased to reign. The parliament passed various laws of resumption, by 1, 5, 6, 7, and 8 Henry IV., to recover the crown lands. The revenue of Henry V., on account of these resumptions, amounted to 56,966l.

The prayer of the commons of 28 Henry VI. says that he had alienated his lands until his income was but 5000l., and that he was in debt 372,000l. That his household expenses amounted yearly to 24,000l., and enacts that all the grants made from the first of his reign should be resumed; no wonder

the house of York dethroned him. 29 Henry
VI. another resumption was made of the fees of
every frankpledge, guilds, and profits granted by
him ; this was again re-enacted by 33 Henry VI. A
most sweeping resumption was made by 1 Edward
IV., which enacts that all lands should be resumed from
20 Richard II. ; this was endeavoured to be set aside
by 3 and 4 Edward IV., and that the resumption
should only take place from 4th March, 1461, and it
makes a prodigious number of reservations ; but the
7 Edward IV. declares the resumption shall be
made, and the king thanked the commons, who
it seems had bestirred themselves for the resumption ; there is, therefore, little doubt that the
Yorkists were popular, and that the people did
not altogether side with them on account of primo-
genitureship, but because they promised a resumption which the Lancastrians, or court party, were
unwilling to adopt. The reformation which had
been begun by Henry V., as to church property,
was effected by Elizabeth's father, Henry VIII.,
and nearly the whole of the abbey lands was seized
by the crown, amounting to £131,607 6s. 4d. per
annum, and though large grants were made by the
policy of Henry to the nobles, to concur with this
great change, yet the revenue of the crown and
church lands held by Elizabeth amounted to 188,1971.
4s. an income which made her set the nobles
at defiance, and dictate to her parliaments. Though
the nobles were thus subdued, the lower classes, for

more than one hundred and eighty years, had been extremely feverish, and seemed determined to crush the higher classes. The example of the Netherlands and that of France by the Jaques Bon Hommes had been imitated by Wat Tyler, followed up by Jack Cade, and Kit the tanner; and lastly, even in the time of Elizabeth, destroyed the inclosures and declared the land should be *one common*, determined Elizabeth to conciliate the lower classes and ameliorate their condition; this certainly was done but slowly; but then it was done, and the working classes began to be considered as men having rights: a very great mistake seems to have been generally received, that the number of persons employed in manufactures were not numerous in the days of Elizabeth, as will plainly be perceived by any per-son who will take the trouble to read the various places mentioned by acts of parliament, where various trades were carried on.

The 5th Eliz. cap. 4, is now the foundation of the laws of England, respecting masters and their servants; but the greater part of whose enactments have become obsolete and inapplicable, from a change of time and circumstances. This Act has been more patched than all the Acts, (excepting revenue Acts,) put together; clause after clause has been repealed, till it requires a great deal of time and attention to discover what part is law, and what is not. The Act consists of 48 Sections; and, as have before been observed, repeals all former Acts

as to hiring, Wages, &c. 3rd Sec. enumerates 40
trades, and declares they shall not be hired for less
than a year. 4th Requires all unmarried persons,
(with certain exceptions as to property, &c.) being
of the aforementioned Crafts (Trades,) upon request of any person to serve. 5th No persons
shall put away his said servant before the time of
hiring is expired, without showing cause before one
justice ; nor servant depart without shewing cause.
This clause we have re-enacted in the new Bill, as
it has been the practice for masters in manufactures,
&c. to hire servants for a great length of time, who
are compelled, by 6th Geo. 3rd, cap. 25th, to serve,
but the master frequently dischargeth them at
a moment's notice, without assigning any cause.
If a master hires a servant for a length of period,
he prevents him from making any other advantageous bargain until that period is transpired ; and
he ought to be compelled to keep that servant, who
hires for the sake of the employment: to discharge
him without cause is to defraud him. 6th Section
enacts, that such servants shall not quit without
a quarter's warning. This wholesome custom is
kept up by gentlemen with their servants, but is
quite obsolete in trades. Sec. 7th requires all
persons within the age of 12 and 60 years, excepting gentlemen of 40s. yearly, mariners,
apprentices, carriers, husbandmen, or colliers or
mines, not having a convenient term, to be hired by
any person making a request, *in the same shire,*

E

obsolete. 8th Sec. Any master, &c. putting away his servant without cause, forfeits 40s: this clause we retain as far as it goes, as to masters. 9th Section, Servants leaving service before expiration of time, or not giving a quarter's warning, or refusing to serve for the wages rated by justices, to be committed. The spirit of this we retain. 10th Section, None of the said servants shall depart from the town or hundred where they last served, without a Testimonial signed by the Mayor or Constable, and two Householders, which Testimonial shall be registered by the Parson or Vicar. (so that we find the custom of passports has prevailed in England, and is now the law.) 11th Sec. No person shall be hired without his Testimonial, and shall be imprisoned if he does not produce it; and if in 21 days he cannot procure it, shall be treated as a vagabond. *This is now the law.* 12th Persons hired in husbandry, by the day or week, shall work 15 hours per day, deducting $2\frac{1}{2}$ hours for meals and sleep. 13th Sec. Persons who shall undertake to make any ship, house, or mill, or any work taken by gross or piece, and shall depart before finishing, unless for non-payment of wages, shall be imprisoned one month, and fined five pounds. This is altered by 12th Geo. 1st, 22nd Geo. 2nd, 6th Geo. 3rd, and imprisons, whether wages is paid or not. We have amended this clause to 14 days' notice to quit, and master to summons for damages, if he can prove them; this clause has been much abused, as in many businesses they never finish their work, as the nature of the employment is such, that they are compelled to begin one before they finish another, as wheelrights, japanners, and an infinite number of trades; therefore, if any dispute ariseth respecting the amount of wages, and a strike or turn-out commences, or men leave their work, having words, the master prosecutes them for leaving their work unfinished; very few prosecutions have been made to effect under the combination Acts, but hundreds have been made under this law, and the labourer or workman can never be free, unless this law is modified; the combination Act is nothing: it is the law which regards the finishing of work, which masters employ to harass and keep down the wages of their work people; unless this is modified nothing is done, and by repealing the combination Acts, you leave the workman, in 99 cases out of 100, in the same state you found him,—at the mercy of his master.

The clauses which restrain the master from discharging his servant before the time of hiring is expired, and suffering the servant to leave his employ on giving fourteen days' notice, are considered the very key stones of the Bill, without their enactment the servant will not be free, and his master will always have it in his power to oppress him; as to the inconvenience the master may suffer, not one case occurs in a thousand where the master will sus-

tain any other injury than being compelled to raise
the wages of servants ; as for the work being spoilt
it seldom occurs ; the finishing is a branch of the
system to compel a man to work for low wages ;
in the feudal times, it was meant as a restraint upon
their bargains, and it is the greatest restraint that
can well be conceived : a number of servants, on
account of change of trade, &c. wish to leave their
master, if he will not give them fair wages ; he says,
I cannot prevent you from leaving WHEN you have
finished your work ; but if a man leaves before he
has finished, a gaol is his doom: instead of acting
with one impulse, to compel him to give fair wages,
some must stay a month, some two months, and
perhaps some leave and are made what the master
calls examples of, by being imprisoned ; and the
poor fellows, perhaps, deprived of what little public spirit and intellect is amongst them, by impri-
soning the most bold amongst them, are compelled
to drag along at the reduced wages; for this happens
in the case of reductions, as well as advances : thus,
a master gives notice that he shall abate the wages ;
the men wish to quit his employ: No, says he, I
pay you the price for what you have engaged to do,
but every man that leaves his work before it is
finished, he knows the consequence ; I will imprison
him. Perhaps out of 100, 10 can leave instantly,
and the rest are compelled to supply his market,
for a week, a month, or even two months, while he
can take his measures to learn or procure hands, or

tamper weak minds, as to constant employment, &c.
while he effects a division, causeth a part to submit,
and induceth the other masters to follow his example. This case has been verified a hundred
times. The combination Act is difficult to convict
upon; one of the workmen must turn traitor, to
convict; but the neglecting the work it easy proved;
therefore, if you continue the Combination Acts, the
workmen would regard them in a great measure as
waste paper, but suffer them to leave, on giving
notice, and you set them free at once.

14th Sec. The same punishment for leaving the
Queen's work. 15th, The Justices of the Peace are
directed, within their respective Counties, together
with the Sheriffs and the Mayors, &c. to meet in
Sessions, within six weeks after Easter, and call
unto them grave and discreet persons, having respect to the plenty or scarcity of the time, to fix the
rate of wages of Labourers and Artificers, by the
year, week, day, or otherwise, with meat and drink,
or without; and shall cause the same *to be certified
to the Chancery, who shall cause the same to be laid
before the Privy Council,* who shall cause it to be
printed and sent down to the several Counties, to
be proclaimed in open market days, before Michael-
mas. It will be seen that Elizabeth kept a checque
upon the Justices, as they had to refer to the Privy
Council, before it was printed and sent down for
Proclamation.

And in the Scottish law, the same enactment was

made by Mary, queen of Scots, at the same period.
This course was pursued during the whole reign of
Elizabeth, until the next reign of James the First,
when the privy council declined the trouble and
appointed commissioners to fix the rate of wages ;
during the reign of Charles I. a commissioner was
appointed, but the protector Cromwell gave a
death-blow to the system, and from that time,
though the demon of low wages, that bane to the
prosperity and wealth of states has often attempted
to raise its head, yet, until the late war, public opinion, in a great measure, kept the happiness-de-
stroying monster down.   An attempt was made by
7 George I., cap. 13, to fix the rates of tailors'
wages in the metropolis, which was enacted that
tailors should be paid only two shillings and six-
pence per day; this was again enacted by 8 George
III., cap. 17, and tailors' wages were again fixed
to keep the wages low ; these two acts have not
been repealed, they are still law, though it is notorious that tailors' wages in London are now five
shillings and six-pence per day.   The bill which is
now before the House repeals both these acts.
The year 1773 produced a new æra, and marks
the strange vicissitudes of human events.   The
laws which had been heretofore so obnoxious to
the workmen and artificers, were now in the most
clamorous manner demanded by them.   The silk
weavers in Spitalfields, disgusted at the avaricious
conduct of their masters, determined to throw

themselves into the hands of the magistrates to fix the rate of their wages ; force, both open and secret, were used for that purpose. The work of those weavers who were working beneath the usual rates were cut from the looms, the masters' looms and property were destroyed ; the minister was surrounded in his house, and compelled to promise to pass a bill to empower the magistrates of London, Southwark, and Middlesex, to fix the rate of wages ; the most dreadful riots took place; soldiers were shot, and several of the cutters were executed. This violence lasted several years, and peace and tranquillity were not restored until the act 13 George III., cap. 68, was passed. What a change of events and public opinion !*

From 1349 till the æra of Cromwell, 1649, the artificers and labourers had run the risk of being branded with red hot irons and treated as felons rather than submit to the rates fixed by magistrates, and then in little more than a century they become outrageous for the magistrates to have the power sooner than their masters ; they were by no means singular in their notions. In 1779, the stocking makers of Nottingham, Leicester, and Derby, and in fact of England and Scotland, applied to parliament for an act to raise the rate of their wages, and fix them by law.

In 1808, the weavers of Lancashire and its

---

* See debates on the petitions of master silk-weavers, respecting these acts.

neighbourhood, as well as those of Northumberland and Cumberland, whose wages had been reduced, became extremely clamorous for the magistrates to fix the rate of their wages ; serious riots ensued, and large bodies of troops were marched to keep the public peace, and protect the magistrates for not putting the laws in force. " The journeymen, and some of the masters in Manchester and Glasgow, applied to the court of King's Bench for a writ of mandamus, to compel the magistrates to fix the rate of wages, according to 5 Elizabeth, cap. 14, sect. 15, and 1 Jac. 1, cap. 6 ; this writ was delayed for years, and at last, when every subterfuge had been tried by the courts, down came lord Sidmouth to the house of lords, in 1813, with a bill to repeal the 5 Elizabeth, and 1 Jac. I., and all acts passed by the Scotch parliament to fix the rate of wages : the grounds of his lordship's motion was, that their lordships were too enlightened to let them remain upon the statute book any longer;"* since which period every indirect effort has been made to repeal the 13 George III., cap. 68, and the legislators of the present day seem as much alarmed at the laws for fixing the rates of wages as the journeymen were, in the fourteenth, fifteenth, and sixteenth centuries, at having them fixed by the magistrates. The motive in the legislators is the

* Why did not Mr. Ricardo and Mr. Huskison then join with his lordship, and repeal the object of their astonishment, the Spital-fields' acts, as well as the above acts ?

57

same, to keep the wages low; they are apprehen-
sive, if the Magistrates had the power to fix the
rate of wages, that they would raise them ; in this
opinion they are, it is believed, right, as it is contrary to common justice and humanity to expect
that any deliberative body of men, not immediately
interested, would award such a low rate of wages,
as that now given, for making of goods in a great
number of the principal manufactures in this kingdom. Nothing can equal the misery which the
slow and aged workmen suffer ; and this may be
relied upon, that the rate of wages now given will
never content the majority of the workmen, and it
will always be subject to serious riots and disturbances upon the slightest occasions ; and, in fact, to
the most serious and alarming emigrations which
are taking place every day to France. Those workmen who now emigrate are superior workmen, who
are preparing the way for more general emigrations.
The extensive and vigorous prohibitory system,
adopted by the continental states, are extremely
favourable to these emigrations.*

Section 16 merely directs, that if they, the magistrates, continue the old rates, they must certify
the same to the chancery. Sec. 17.—Justices not
attending to fix the rate, forfeit 10l. 18.—Any
person giving greater wages than contained in pro-

* Vide Ship-builders' petition, presented a few days ago respecting emigration of workmen, and praying a repeal of the
Acts.

clamation, to be imprisoned ten days and forfeit 5l.
19.—Persons taking *greater wages*, to be imprisoned twenty-one days. Sec. 20.—All promise
of greater wages, &c., to be void and of none effect.
Sec. 21.—If any servant shall make any affray
upon his master or overseer, shall be imprisoned
one year, or shall be punished in any other manner
so as not to extend to life or limb. This arbitrary
enactment is made transportation by 12 George I.,
cap. 84, and by 22 George II., cap. 27, in certain
manufactures, by 6 George III., cap. 25, it is included in misbehaviour and imprisonment for not
less than one nor more than three months. Sec.
22 directs, that any handicraftsman may be compelled to work in harvest time ; this is obsolete,
and useless *now* to re-enact. Sec. 23.—Any person not having harvest work in his own county, on
procuring testimonial may remove to another. Sec.
24.—Women above twelve years, and under forty,
may be compelled to serve. Sec. 25.—Any person being an householder, occupying half a plough
of land, may take apprentices in husbandry above
ten and under eighteen years of age, as they can
agree. We interfere not with apprentices. Sec.
26.—Any person being an householder, and twenty-
four years of age, in any town corporate, may take
the son of any freeman an apprentice, not being a
labourer or employed in husbandry, according to
the practice of the city of London, so as the term
of such apprenticeship does not expire before such

apprentice *is twenty-four years of age !!!* Sec. 27.
—Merchants trading beyond the sea, mercers,
drapers, goldsmiths, ironmongers, embroiderers, or
clothiers, not to take apprentices or servants unless
their parents shall have 40s per year!!! This
is law now ; twenty-eight inhabitants of a market
town being artificers, twenty-four years of age,
may take the children of any other artificer to be
an apprentice ; this was a great condescension from
the 7 Henry IV., cap. 17, which says, that their
parents shall have land to the amount of 20s. Sec.
29 merely repeats sec. 27. Sec. 30 enumerates
twenty-six trades, as smiths, carpenters, masons,
talkers, fallers, thatchers, &c. who might take apprentices, although their parents have not lands.
Sec. 31.—No person after the first of May, 1563,
shall set any person at work in any of the mysteries
or arts *now used* in England or Wales, unless he
shall have served seven years apprenticeship, upon
pain of 40s per month. In 1809, 10, 11, and 12,
the mechanics of the metropolis set themselves seriously at work to put this enactment in full force ;
they were supported in a very vigorous manner by
the country mechanics, but this section was repealed
by a bill brought in by an honourable member, in
1812, for which, it is said, he received several
pieces of plate from the masters of several manufacturing towns.*

---

* Mr. Sergeant Onslow.

The repeal of this enactment is one of great consequence and weight, and has more to do with the morals of the country than that honourable member is aware of. It ought to have been amended; it is a subject of vital importance in the education and restraint of youth, and it is now left open to a boy, to be apprenticed or not, that is, put under salutary controul, until he is twenty-one years of age.

Section 32.—No person shall take an apprentice as a woollen cloth weaver in Cumberland, Westnorland, Lancashire, and Wales, unless his parents shall have freehold to the amount of 60s. yearly, on pain of 40s per month ; repealed very properly. Sec. 33.—Cloth makers, fullers, sheermen, weavers, tailors, and shoe makers, shall, for every three apprentices, have one journeyman, and for every apprentice above three, one journeyman. This has been re-enacted for various trades, again and again. Sec. 34.—Not to prejudice worsted weavers in Norwich. Sec. 35.—If any person shall be required by any householder having half a plough of land, or using any art or mystery, to serve, he may be committed until he will serve (obsolete) ; masters evil intreating their apprentices, justices may take order therein, or apprentices misconducting themselves, in either case four justices in sessions may cancel the indenture. Sec. 36.—No apprentice to be compelled to serve, being twenty-one years of age. 37.—The justices required to see this statute enforced without favour or affection; the justices now-a-days, in many instances, do not feel themselves bound to act according to law, and frequently without assigning any cause, refuse to act. Sec. 38.—Justices putting this act in force, allowed five shillings per day, but not to exceed pay for three days—to be paid out of the fines of the statute!!! 39 Regulates fines. Sec. 40.—Not to injure London and Norwich, as to apprentices. Sec. 41.—All indentures or covenants contrary to the act, void, and forfeit 10l. Sec. 43.—Apprentices, though within twenty-one years, to be bound by their indentures. Sec. 44.—The inhabitants of Godalming may take apprentices. Sec. 45.—Receivers of fines appointed. Sec. 46.—Not to extend to retainings made before passing the act. 47.—Servants fleeing out of their shires may be apprehended by warrant. 48.—High constables may hold their petty sessions and statute sessions. Some faint remains of these statutes yet remain, for hiring servants in husbandry, in the northern and midland counties, and they were, we thought, the origin of some of the fairs round London.

We have thus been minute in describing the 5 Elizabeth, cap. 4, because it is the only general code which regulates masters and servants ; all the other parts of the code of laws only relate to particular trades or descriptions of men, or to particular offences.

After a period of two hundred and sixty years, a code of laws is presented to the House, for the regulation of the very extensive and fundamental interests of masters and their servants. It is really astonishing to see how the 5 Elizabeth has been patched and maimed; a single section is altered without naming the original, or repealed by a single section thirty or forty years after another section is repealed; and, again, in the same time another man, who would be affronted if you denied him the right of being called a legislator, repeals another solitary clause; but the object of this present attempt is to repeal the whole together, and form a new code applicable, as it is hoped it will prove, to present times and circumstances; they may be put into the hands of journeymen and servants, who may know by what laws they are bound, and not to have to hunt in thirty or forty volumes for forty-five acts of parliament to know what is law, or as to what they may do or what they may not do. The ignorance which pervades the working classes as to what laws they are bound by, is deplorable indeed; and, in fact, what little they do know, they continually ask one another, "Well, but are you sure it is not *repealed?*" This may justly be considered to be the bitterest sarcasm that can be uttered upon modern British legislation.

Having entered so freely on the effects of the preceding act of Elizabeth, little need be said of the concluding part of her reign, which certainly merited that degree of popularity which she obtained from the working classes. 5 Elizabeth, cap. 7,

prohibits the same as 1 Richard III., a number of
manufactured articles. Chapter 20 enacts, that
any persons joining with the gypsies, shall be
guilty of felony without clergy. The 8 Elizabeth,
cap. 7, and 14 Elizabeth, cap. 52, directs the
cottoners of Shrewsbury to pay in money, under
pain of losing their franchise. 8 Elizabeth, cap.
11, endeavours to prevent the making felt hats,
which had deprived the cap makers of employment,
whereby a number of towns had been brought to
desolation. By the 13 Elizabeth, cap. 8, the interest of money was fixed at ten per cent. Chap.
19 directs every person above seven years of age
to wear a cap of *wool knit* on the Sabbath, upon
pain to forfeit, for every day not wearing, 3s. 4d.
with certain exceptions!!! The 14 Elizabeth,
cap. 5, enacts that all *vagabonds* shall be grievous-
ly whipped, and burned through the gristle of the
right ear, an inch; and being above eighteen, shall
suffer death as a felon, unless some one will take
him to service for two years ; if he fall into it a
third time, to be executed as a felon.* The 5 Elizabeth, cap. 3, is the first compulsory law to the
poor, which was improved by 14 Elizabeth, cap. 5,
sec. 2. By 31 Elizabeth, cap. 5, and 43 Elizabeth, cap. 1, these poor laws in a great measure
freed the kingdom from vagabonds, and the ame-

---

* Would not this clause be very applicable to the present
laws regarding *poachers ?*

lioration of the condition of the poor completed it. Low wages are now filling the manufactural districts with desperadoes who will not work.

Elizabeth, though arbitrary in her notions of prerogative, was extremely fond of popularity, which she enjoyed in a great degree from the working classes, having ameliorated their condition by increasing the rate of wages, and at the same time improved the condition of the great mass of her subjects. The odious system of granting, by the prerogative of the crown, the exclusive right to noblemen, &c. of buying, selling, and making various commodities, was in a great measure abolished; and her successor, James, put the finishing stroke to *monopolies*,* by 21 Jac. 1, cap. 3, which expressly forbids the granting of Letters Patent, &c. to any person but true and real inventors.

Fixing the rate of wages by the justices was still adopted; and, 1 Jac. cap. 6, the Privy Council ceased to exercise a control over them. Commissions of gentlemen also were appointed, to enforce these rates, and the Stuarts soon became unpopular.

The turbulent reign of Charles the First gave the *parliament* but little opportunity to attend to restrictions on servants, and as they were *opposed* to the *court*, they did not chuse to make themselves *odious* by *oppressing the labourer.*

---

* What would they have said to the present provisions of the game bill?

The civil wars between the Parliament and the crown, effectually broke and destroyed the chains which had been placed around the artizan and the labourer for three centuries, and left him *free* to demand his *own price* for his services. Neither Cromwell nor his generals interfered with wages and servants, and it was during the short reign of that great man that the world saw, for the first time, *the labouring and productive classes treated as men*, free from tyrannical laws, and protected by a liberal government, which, however *faulty* in some other respects, had the enviable glory of *increasing the happiness of the most necessary and the most useful part of mankind,*—the artizans and labourers. England, from this moment, began to tower over the nations of the earth. Her population, treated as *men*, soon began to bestir themselves; invention succeeded invention, improvement in every branch of employ or manufacture soon appeared; the whole population became industrious. The Netherlands and Brabant, whose manufactures exceeded the then known nations, soon gave way to Britain; France soon found a rival whose productions eclipsed her, and the Spaniard, and his once boasted manufactories, soon became paralized by the superior fabrics of his hitherto crippled rivals. The population of Italy and Lombardy were doomed to idleness; the ingenuity and industry of the western island had superseded her productions in most goods but the manufacture of silks. Even in this de-

F

partment, the throwing of silk, the English began now a rivalry. It is true, that many restraints yet existed; such as the corporations refusing to let any work, in their respective trades, but a member; the same existed in various towns, but these disputes were amongst themselves, the hand of power did not interfere, they were comparatively harmless; Charles the second followed the liberal principle of the times, as only two Acts which relates to artizans and servants were made during his reign, 13th and 14th Car. 2, cap. 15, and 23 Car. 2, cap. 6. They both relate to silk throwsters; they limit the number of apprentices, &c.; and what is very remarkable, are the first Acts which punish servants for embezzling their master's property, in materials intrusted to them. These statutes for punishing persons for embezzlement of materials, have increased very much since that period, several of which are mere repetitions of former statutes. The 8th and 9th Will. 3, cap. 36, which prohibits the importation of lustrings and alamodes, repeats the two Acts of Charles 2nd, and extends to receivers.—The 1st Anne, sec. 2, cap. 18, extends the punishment of persons embezzling and receiving materials, to woollen, linen, fustian, cotton, and iron manfactures. This was made perpetual by 9 Anne, cap. 30. The 9 Geo. 1st, cap. 27, punishes journeymen shoe-makers for embezzlement; the 13 Geo. 1st, cap. 23, relates to reeling false yarn, and to using frauds in

the woollen manufacture. The provisions of the
1st Anne, by the 13th Geo. 2, cap. 8, generally to
embezzlement of leather, without repealing 9th Geo.
1st, cap. 27. The 22d Geo. II., cap. 27, con-
denses all these Acts without repealing them, and
extends the provisions only to hats, woollen, linen,
fustian, cotton, iron, leather, hemp, flax, mohair, and
silk manufactures, and gives the power to magistrates to issue search warrants to recover embezzled materials. The 1st Anne, and the 13th Geo.
II. directs double damages to be recovered, when
materials are embezzled ; but the 22nd Geo. II.,
cap. 27th, directs a positive imprisonment. The
enactments of 1st Anne, and 13th Geo. II. are
both very objectionable, partial, and cruel: they
direct, that if the servant cannot pay the double,
or in case of second offence, quadruple damage,
he is to be whipped in the prison for the first, and
in the market-place for the second, offence ; thus
brutalizing the population, and punishing the poor
man with a large family, who is unable to pay, and
letting the more fortunate, but perhaps guiltier
rogue escape, because he or his friends have got
money to save his back from a punishment, the disgrace and ignominy of which operates very differ-
ently on various minds : to some persons 'twas a
species of punishment from which they never recovered ; while others, regarding only the corporeal
pain, laughed at it. The 22nd Geo. II. has been
construed to leave the offence optional as to whip-

ping ; only, in case of persons receiving embezzled materials, and not paying the penalty, the public whipping is imperative. There is a very singular and partial clause in 22 Geo. II., which gives the right of appeal to the Sessions to the receiver, but denies it to the servant. The injustice, as well as impolicy of this, is very manifest.

The 27th Geo. 2, cap. 7, extends the punishment of embezzlement to clocks and watches. A *repetitiory*, as far as regards the woollen manufacture, was made by 14 Geo. 3, cap. 25, and was again repeated by 15 Geo. 3, cap 14. But the general law for the punishing embezzlement is by 17 Geo. 3, cap. 56. This Act punisheth persons embezzling materials, for the first offence, not less than 14 days, nor more than three months ; and retains the whipping, if the Justice shall think fit ; that is, give him 3 months' imprisonment, and if he shall think fit, cause him to be publickly whipped, which is equal to two years' imprisonment, to a man of any sensibility, and next to the punishment of death to many. It is tantamount to banishment from the neighbourhood. It should be observed, that by 17 Geo. 3, not returning materials in 8 days after notice, is considered as proof of embezzlement. The employer is not to prove that the workman has disposed of them, he only proves that he has not received them from the servant. There is no provision for waste in the enactment, for accident, for theft, or any other cause; but, like Shylock, the master demands his materials, and if they are not produced, and the very same materials which he delivered, the servant may, and has been imprisoned and whipped. In some districts, to the honour of the magistrates, this brutal sentence of whipping is seldom directed; and in many manufacturing districts never. In the silk manufactures, whipping has been frequently resorted to. By the Act, the punishment for receiving is increased; but by a singular provision, the receiver, if directed to be whipped, is only to be imprisoned three days, whilst the poor servant may have 3 months and a whipping!!! Notwithstanding which anomaly, (which most probably was an oversight,) this Act is very properly directed to punish and prevent the receiving of embezzled materials; but at the same time it enacts a most extraordinary provision; for the first offence the Act directs not less than £20, nor more than £40 fine, and in default of payment, not less than 3, nor more than 6, months' imprisonment. For the second offence, the Justices are restrained from proceeding to conviction, but are directed to commit the offender to the sessions *unless he can find* bail: and then, strange to say, if he is convicted by the sessions, though the penalty is increased to not less than £50 nor more than £100, still the imprisonment is the same, in default of payment, as to the first offence. The operation of which clause is, that persons are not prosecuted for a second offence, on account of the delay and expense. This law, as it now stands, has very little effect in preventing the practice of receiving embezzled materials, as, in most large manufacturing districts, there are numbers of unprincipled masters, who make a regular practice of buying embezzled materials, not from the workmen, but from an agent, who has purchased from the workman, or from the thief, (as stealing materials ready-made has become very prevalent in the midland districts.) When his agent is committed, he keeps him well in prison, as a matter of policy, sooner than pay the penalty, to harass the prosecutor, who loses the material, 20s. 6d. fees if convicted before Justices, but if convicted at sessions, the costs of the counsel, attorney, court fees, witnesses, &c. will amount to near £10, and many masters consider the remedy worse than the disease, by prosecuting. In fact, this description of offenders laugh at the idea of being convicted, as they are well maintained in prison, and they know that they have inflicted a loss upon the prosecutor nearly equal to the penalty ; the public will perhaps scarcely believe that they have their committees, to defend themselves, &c. and that, in one town, not containing 40,000 inhabitants, there are 200 persons, masters and agents, not including hawkers, who practise this business of dealing in embezzled materials. No one practice has done so much injury to the manufacturing classes as this, receiving embezzled materials, as the moral honesty of the population is by this means sapped, and a quantity of goods is continually, in flat trades, brought into the market, beneath *prime cost* of lawfully obtained materials and the labour. This has always a tendency to reduce the price of labour, as the honest master cannot reduce the price of the material, to meet this practice, he therefore reduces the price of labour, which, though by no means a remedy, yet it is an expedient constantly resorted to. This Act directs the magistrate to issue warrants to search for embezzled materials. An information is laid, the public house is searched (for these people have regular well-known public houses which they frequent openly,) the materials are seized, the warrant is directed to search the house of the landlord, who is to give a satisfactory account how he came by the same; he produces the person who brought them to his house; there is no proof against the landlord, the information *is against him*, he is consequently discharged, and the law is evaded. Sometimes more than 100 workmen will attend upon one such house in one day, to dispose of embezzled materials, they having substituted grease, damp-salt, alum, soap, &c. &c. for materials.

On the other hand, there have not been wanting unprincipled masters, who have delivered short weight, and have loaded their materials with wet, &c. For these evils there has hitherto been no remedy but by *construction*, in the case of a servant, and no remedy against the master. The 17th Geo. 3rd, contains a sweeping clause, inapplicable and unjust towards the servant: it says that all the provisions of the Act shall be equally applicable to the tools and implements, drugs and ingredients, the same as materials delivered; that is, the master, may give his servant 8 days' notice to return his tools, or ingredients, and if he does not submit, he may have three months' imprisonment, and be publicly whipped. Nothing is so common, as for servants to spend their pounds, and lose month after month, in making experiments for the improvement of their machinery: and the master, as the law now stands, can demand the result of all his ingenuity, his perhaps important discovery in machines, in eight days, and leave him to the unavailing regret of having so misspent his time and genius. It is in mechanics as in every other department of art, that nothing is so difficult as to discover a new method, but yet nothing is so easy as to imitate it, when once it is seen accomplished. The workmen are in general the operative mechanists; the masters in general are capitalists, who do not understand the principles upon which their machinery or tools are constructed; and, consequently, the workmen, now having no law to protect them, in losing their time and money to improve their machinery, as to fresh patterns and fabricks, &c. in a great measure cease to improve. In a great many of the principal manufactures in the kingdom, in which machinery are employed, to secure the workmen, in such cases, a fair renumeration by law, would be a master stroke of policy. The effect would be much greater than the privilege of patents. A workman is, generally speaking, a man without *capital* ; his tools, though not his own property, he considers in a great measure his *estate*, when he has applied any new invention to them; and he feels, when deprived of his tools and his improvement, the same bitter pang as a nobleman would, should his estate be overwhelmed by the sea, or swallowed up by an earthquake,

By the same Act it is enacted, that masters may, at all seasonable hours in the day-time, inspect their materials: that is, inspect their materials upon the machines; or in other words, go and see if he has an ingenious workman. He makes a new article, that he may put the whole of his workmen on, with the discovery, or improvement, without allowing the ingenious servant any thing for his discovery. This has been, in many instances, a great bar to improvement; as, unless ingenious men can have tools of their own, they dare not improve, on account of their insecurity ; and as to tools of their own, it is a well-known fact, that men of the greatest genius and talents have not been remarkable, in any science, or any age, for their provident conduct for the morrow. Receivers of stolen goods are generally considered the greatest pests of society; and receivers of embezzled materials, are certainly not the less so. Yet, by 17th Geo. 3rd, cap. 56, sec. 3rd, it is impossible to form a conviction, to convict one species of offence. There are two overt Acts described; one, for receiving materials, knowing them to be embezzled; and the other, for receiving materials from a person, knowing him to be employed, without having the consent of the person employing him. Now, if it should so happen, (which it generally does,) that the person should stand in the double capacity of disposing of embezzled materials, and being a person employed, it is impossible to draw up the conviction right: if you charge them with receiving from a workman employed, the conviction is squashed, because the receiver knew they were embezzled, and, if embezzled, then it ought to have been from a person employed. This oversight is remedied in the silk manufacture, by 32nd Geo. 3rd, cap. 44. The present Common Sergeant of the city of London, when Recorder of a large manufacturing town, was compelled to quash no less than four informations, laid against notorious offenders, at *one sessions*, upon this ground.

This Act directs an appeal in all cases, and in what manner the appeal shall be made; but, as it does not repeal the appeal clause, 22nd Geo. 2nd, cap. 27, it is held doubtful which course the defendant may take.

As far as regards the hardship of demanding tools on a short notice, this was alleviated in one particular manufacture, namely, the framework-knitted, or hosiery manufacture. By the 28th Geo. 3rd, cap. 55, which enacts, that masters demanding their frames, &c. must give fourteen days' notice, and directs a fine of 20s, on non compliance; and if, in 6 days afterwards, the frames are not delivered up, then the workman is liable to not less than one, nor more than three months' imprisonment. No appeal is allowed, and no provision is then made how the master is to recover his property; and unless he proceeds, *de novo*, after the term of imprisonment is expired, which is contrary to the first principle of law and equity, to punish *twice* for one offence. As the law now stands, a workman, damaging his work wilfully, may be punished; but, damaging his tools there is no law to punish him, unless he is proceeded against capitally, *for breaking and destroying*, which certainly was not contemplated by the legislature, which only meant to punish persons damaging machinery, where force was employed.

Seventy years had elasped from the death of Cromwell, before any general restrictive law was made respecting servants; but in 1727, an Act was passed to prevent unlawful combinations of workmen employed in the woollen manufactures. The 2nd and 3rd Edw. 6th, cap. 15, had not been repealed, it is but fair to presume that its dreadful and cruel operations had become obsolete. The 12th Geo. 1st, cap. 34, declares all contracts, by laws, or agreements, made by journeymen weavers, or wool combers, for regulating the said trade, altering the usual hours of work, &c. illegal, and null and void. Journeymen making such contracts, &c.

to be imprisoned and kept to hard labour, for any time not exceeding three months; or if they shall leave their work, (without shewing cause before two Justices) or depart before the time of hiring is expired, the same punishment is directed; or, if they shall wilfully *damnify, spoil, or destroy* their work, the Justice is empowered to levy double the value on their goods: and if sufficient effects cannot be found, the like punishment.

This is the first statute which directs the recovery of wages according to the contract of the parties, and forbids the payment of wages otherwise than in money. The 4th Edw. IV., and the 8th Eliz. forbids the practice; and the former statute directs treble the amount of the wages to be levied, but they do not contain powers to levy wages generally. This Act directs the wages to be recovered, if not paid in money, *according to the full price agreed on,* by distress and sale; and in default of distress, six months' imprisonment, unless the wages were sooner paid or satisfied. In addition to which, it inflicts the penalty of ten pounds; and though it directs distress and sale for the recovery of the penalty, yet, in case of no effects, NO *punishment* is directed, which is very singular. The two last clauses are highly penal; they direct that if any master shall receive any bodily hurt, for not complying with any such bye-laws or regulations, or if any letter or message shall be sent, threatening to destroy his property, such persons sending such letters, &c. shall be adjudged guilty of felony, and be transported for 7 years. The last clause makes it death, without benefit of clergy, to break or destroy machines, &c. used in the woollen-cloth manufacture, or frame-work knitted woollen manufactures.

What could be the cause for such severe enactments, is but little known : historians are generally *silent* in what concerns "the short but simple annals of the *poor*." Whether it arose from disputes respecting wages, or from being paid in goods, is now, perhaps, impossible to determine ; perhaps both : at all events the disputes must have run very high, as it is fair to presume that the machines of the masters were destroyed,—that threatening letters were sent, and that the masters and workmen had arranged themselves into two hostile parties ; and the law is certainly conceived with some degree of wisdom and candour, as, while it protects the master from violence, it compels him, in some measure, to be just ; but it does not prevent combinations of *masters, which are generally the forerunners of these disorders.* If the dispute originated in paying otherwise than in money, it is not surprising that the workmen proceeded to great lengths in violence, as the oppression to the operative workman is intolerable. This practice has, in almost every instance where it has been carried on to any extent, caused riots and disturbances ; for instance, the Luddites in the midland counties,—the riots in

Staffordshire and Wales, all owed their origin to this cruel system, which takes from the operative workman the right of providing his own necessaries, and effectually cuts him off from society, as the master decides which way he is to dispose of his wages, and he can only supply himself to his own wishes by making large sacrifices of the goods delivered to him, by selling them beneath the real value ; his immediate necessity, and want of capital, induces him to sell, and, if the practice becomes general, he soon loses the market, as where every one has something to sell of similar descriptions, there are plenty of sellers, and cannot but be few buyers.

In 1748, the first general law (20 Geo. II., cap. 14) was passed to enable servants *in general* to recover wages. By this Act servants in husbandry, &c. can recover 10l., but artificers, handicraftsmen, &c. &c. can only recover 5l., and that too only in 21 days, unless the master chooses to pay sooner ; he may then, upon being pressed to pay, appeal to the Sessions, from the judgment of which Sessions he may obtain a certiorari to the Court of King's Bench, which has been done, all of which to obtain the sum of 5l. It is true, that Justices may give the costs, and if the order is found to be good by the Court of King's Bench, the servant may have his *taxed* costs, that is, about one-half his *real* costs, as the gentlemen who are employed, the Lord knows by whom, and by what law, or by what laws, rules, or regulations they are guided, seldom give a poor caitiff of a plaintiff more than one half his *real* and reasonable costs. If such a workman, then, wishes to recover a week's wages, by the existing law, he must first *pay* the summons and constable, making the order, his witnesses oaths : upon the appeal, his witnesses, attorney, brief, consultation, &c. &c. &c. &c. fee counsel, court fees. In the court of King's Bench, if in the country, lawyer, brief, &c. Town agent attending court three or four terms; two or three counsel's fees; perhaps three refresher fees for each, and their clerks, a couple of consultations, as, from the first to the last, the gentlemen have forgot, from the length of time elapsed; for, without consultations, learned counsel *sometimes forget to read their briefs* till they are in court, and all this gauntlet to be run through with a litigious master, perhaps for 12s. Before a workman now attempts to summons his master, he ought to apply to some charitable person, if such can be found, to lend or give him 200l., or perhaps after all, if he should succeed in bringing it to a hearing, if the justice or his clerk are not prime lawyers, the order, or warrant of distress may be wrong worded; and, by the bye, he has no business to dictate to the Justice how he or his clerk shall word the warrant, or perhaps if he was to attempt to do so, and be a little obstreperous if he thought the warrant was wrong, he might be committed for his sagacity, in telling his worship he did not understand law.

Yes, such is the law in England respecting master and servant; payment of wages is now merely optional. 'Tis idle to think that a poor workman, or even poor workmen, clubbing together, can recover wages through all this turmoil and a two years' suit. If there is any thing left among us of justice or fellow-feeling, this will certainly be altered; it is but justice to say, that an Honourable Member* has brought a Bill into the House, to rectify the grievance, so far as regards the twenty-one days, and to allow the magistrate to order immediate payment, but then there is the appeal, and the dreadful certiorari; the twenty-one days is an evil of slight magnitude; it is the appeal which costs the poor man his money and the certiorari is beyond his reach or his patience.

By the 22nd Geo. II., cap. 27, the provisions of 12th Geo. I, cap. 34, except the *death clause*, were extended to the persons employed in the hat, linen, fustian, cotton, *iron*, leather, fur, hemp, flax, mohair, or silk manufactures; that is, they were prevented from entering into combinations, could recover more than £5 wages, and were not to be paid in goods. By 17th Geo. III. cap. 55, it was extended to hatters, and persons were punished for assisting them. In 1796, by the 36th Geo. III.,

---

* Sir J. Boughey, Baronet, member of parliament for Staffordshire,

cap. 111, the restrictions were extended to paper-
makers. But in 1799, it was extended to workmen
in general. This was repealed in 1800; and the
present Act, 39th and 40th Geo. III., cap. 106,
was enacted ; by the 17th clause, the masters are
liable to a penalty of £20 for combining, and, in
default of effects to be committed, not less than
two, nor more than three months; and the contracts
or agreements are declared void ; that is, a poor
master may be sent to prison, and a master who
employs a great number of persons, who are the
persons who generally *do combine*, are to pay
what to them is a mere flea bite, (£20.) Will any
large or extensive manufacturer be deterred from
a combination, by which he expects to realize thousands, by a fine of £20, from which fine he can
appeal, and remove by certiorari? few instances
have occurred of prosecution of masters under this
clause : one was of the master carpenters in London,
in which the magistrates neglected, or refused to
convict; and the other, the magistrates of Nottingham refused to receive the information, although
the combination was publicly advertised, signed by
four of the parties, declaring that they had agreed
to reduce the wages of their workmen, because, as
the magistrates said, the informant could not tell
where they had met to make the agreement, that
is, in what parish they had met, as the Act directs
part of the penalty to the poor of the parish. The
39th and 40th Geo. III., in the two first sections,

G

merely re-enacts the 12th Geo. I. cap. 34, as to
combinations, and extends the provisions to all
workmen employed in trade or manufactures.
The next section punishes persons for decoying or
intimidating others from working. Section 4, punishes any person by imprisonment, who shall attend
any meeting to raise or alter their wages, &c. or
who shall collect money for that purpose. Section
5th, directs a different punishment for the same
offence; that is, persons paying to such illegal combination, forfeit £10, *and persons collecting, forfeit*
£5, by distress and sale; and, in default of sufficient distress, to be imprisoned for not less than two,
nor more than three, calendar months. Section 6,
7, 8, declare all money subscribed for combinations
of workmen illegal, and directs how it is to be recovered. 9th Sec. compels persons to give evidence,
but indemnifies them from consequences against
themselves. Sec. 10, is the most extraordinary of any
contained in the British Statute Book:—it enacts that
any Justice shall have power to issue his summons,
to any person offending against this Act, appointing
the time and place where such persons are to attend,
before two Justices; who, upon proof, on oath, of
the delivery of such summons, at the place of abode
of the party, such Justices may proceed to conviction, upon proof of such person's absconding. The
persons who drew up the combination Act were
certainly in earnest to crush combinations of workmen, when they erected a summary tribunal *to con-*

demn men unheard, merely because they abscond. The most atrocious of men, in all other cases, have a trial, for the worst of crimes; what would be thought of a court Justice who should proceed to try an offender, even for murder, before he was apprehended; that is, hear his case, proceed to judgment, and hang him when he was caught, without farther hearing. Surely no conscientious man can say, that workmen who may have disputes with their masters ought not to have fair play, and ought to have at least a *summary hearing*. Sec. 11th, gives power to magistrates to summon witnesses, who, if they shall refuse to attend and be examined, may be imprisoned until they will give evidence; that is, as long as the Justices shall think fit. Surely, no man who has the infirmity of passions and prejudices which the best of us are liable to, ought to have such unlimited power. Sec. 12 relates to form of convictions. Sec. 13 directs, that convictions and commitments shall be entered at Quarter Sessions. Sec. 14 provides that the Act shall not take away the powers of Justices given by any other Act. Sec. 15 directs, that if priviledged persons, in any Trade, will not work for *reasonable wages*, &c. one Justice shall have power to license any person to work. Reasonable wages! who is to be the judge of reasonable wages? one Justice, the friend perhaps of the master applying. The wording of this clause almost brings the mind back to the reign of Edw. III., for then the pretext

was *reasonable wages.* Those masters who recom·
mended this enactment, did not provide when wages
should be unreasonably low. Sec. 16 has great
justice; it enacts, that no person, being a master
in the particular trade or business under which a
matter shall be complained of, or referred under the
Act, shall act as a Justice. Most persons will
think that these provisions are severe enough for
the offence contemplated; but prosecutions have
been instituted for combinations contemplated by
this Act, in which the workmen have been indicted
for conspiracy under 33d Edw. I., and have been
imprisoned for two years. This occurred at Manchester, in the case of the cotton spinners striking,
in 1818, for their old wages.

This statute has been in general, a dead letter
upon those artizans upon whom it was intended to
have an effect; namely, the shoe-makers, printers,
paper makers, ship builders, tailors, &c. who have
had their regular societies, and houses of call, as
though no such Act was in existence; and in fact,
it would be almost impossible for many of those
trades to be carried on without such societies, who
are in general, sick and travelling relief societies:
and the roads and parishes would be much pestered
with these travelling trades, who travel from want
of employment, were it not for their societies, who
relieve what they call *tramps.* Those travelling
trades who have not these societies, are compelled
to beg, &c. and frequently commit depredations.

Some of these tramping trades, as they are called, are obliged to travel at times many hundred miles before they can find employment; and they are maintained at their own expense. It is true, that this tramping is in many instances coupled with keeping up the rate of wages, but let any legislator imagine what would be the consequence of hundreds of persons wandering about, seeking for employment who had no fund or society to apply to ; and who must either beg, rob, or apply to the parish where he happened to fall, to be passed home. The chances of detecting these men would be great indeed, whose trade enables them to live any where. Ask military men, who have deserters from these wandering trades, what are the chances against their being again recognized, even when they have been seen, have joined their regiments, and are well known. But how are they to be traced, when a robbery is committed by a distrest man, whose face is scarcely seen? These tramping societies, or trade clubs, are a great benefit to the morals of the country, as they keep a very strict hand upon each other ; and any man who should commit any glaring offence, would be immediately reported, and refused his blank, or ticket, which constitutes him a member of the society, and which he is compelled continually to renew.

It must be admitted that these societies have, in many instances, been extremely galling to many masters, who wish to take advantage of their workmen; as, as soon as any imposition is practised by an individual master, the whole of his workmen leave him. It has been supposed that these societies keep up the price of wages beyond reason: this is not the case. Generally some of these societies have (as all other public bodies do, acting from circumstances,) committed errors; but the wages of many of these trades have been materially lowered, and that by consent of parties, when the masters have *condescended* to take the opinion of the workmen, candidly upon the occasion. It is certainly more than the most generous and forbearing of men can bear, to be compelled, by force, to sacrifice a part of their income, without consulting them upon the subject; and, with an hauteur notice, " I shall reduce your wages, and shall give you only what I think is right," it is no wonder that men who find that they have remedy, which is by leaving their employment, take that remedy.

But if the evil has been slight in the general travelling trades, it has been extensively felt in the general local manufactural trades of the kingdom. It has there been felt as a tremendous millstone round the necks of the local artizan, which has depressed and debased him to the earth: every Act which he has attempted, every measure that he has devised, to keep up or raise his wages, he has been told was illegal: the whole force of the civil power, and influence of his district, has been exerted against him because he was acting illegal; the magistrates,

acting as they believed in unison with the views of
the legislature, to check and keep down wages and
combination, regarded, in almost every instance,
every attempt on the part of the artizan to ameliorate his situation, or support his station in society,
as a species of sedition and resistance of the government; every committee, or active man among them,
was regarded as a turbulent, dangerous instigator,
whom it was necessary to watch and crush if possible.

The masters who were selfish, taking advantage
of this state of things, gradually, in many instances,
and rapid in others, reduced the wages of the operative manufacturers, 'till they were compelled to
apply for parochial relief, to obtain even a bare
subsistence; and this reduction, too, took place in
districts where wages had always been low, and
where it had been difficult for the artizan to obtain
a competent maintenance. The extreme burthen
of the Poor Rates, caused a greater inquiry into the
subject of wages than had been hitherto devoted
to the subject. The landholder, clergy, farmer,
tradesman, and other inhabitants, began to doubt
the policy of taxing themselves to pay the deficit
of wages, for the advantage of a few avaricious
master manufacturers; for it ought in justice to be
stated, that the great majority of the masters, in
some districts, have been decidedly averse to the
extreme reduction of wages which has taken place;
" But then, (as they justly observe,) I cannot afford

to give more than my neighbours carrying on the same business, who would then outrival, undersell me, and take away my business."

The landholders, clergy, and respectable inhabitants of the Borough and County of Leicester, were the foremost to see the gross error of low wages, and the ruinous effects of workpeople being paid part of their wages in Poor Rates, and they very meritoriously set about providing a remedy, which was, to wholly maintain all those persons who could not obtain employment in the hosiery manufactures, at what was termed the Statement price, that is, a list of prices drawn up by the workmen, which, though yet very low, was far above the rate of price given. Subscriptions for this purpose was also forwarded ; the Lord Lieutenant of the County, to his everlasting honour, openly subscribed ; the example was followed by most of the gentlemen of rank in the county ; the pulpit lent its never-failing aid, and the situation of the workmen soon became ameliorated.

The neighbouring county of Nottingham was engaged in the same manufacture, and it became necessary to cause the same wages to be paid in that county. The same feeling for the working classes existed in that county, but the magistrates viewed the transaction with an eye of jealousy and distrust. At first they did not openly oppose the measure, but at length they did not hesitate to declare they should put the laws in force, namely, prosecute under the Combination Act. This they at length did: the workmen's Committee were twice seized, and at length four were convicted by the county magistrates. The workmen, upon appealing to the Sessions, were acquitted, on account of an error in the conviction. It was the intention of the hosiers who prosecuted these poor men, had they been successful with the workmen, to have indicted the Lord Lieutenant, the Mayor, and several of the Aldermen of Leicester, as well as the overseers of the poor, some of the clergy, both of the Establishment and of the Dissenters, for a criminal conspiracy to impede them in their business, and cause their workmen to conspire to raise the rate of their wages. These workmen were prosecuted, in defiance of law, on an anonymous information, in open violation of the Statute of 18 Eliz. cap. 5th, which positively declares, that no man shall be charged on an *anonymous information.*

The inhabitants of Coventry have been placed in a similar predicament, and an indictment for a criminal conspiracy was found by the Grand Jury, for an attempt to prevent a workman from working at a low rate of wages, which rate had been so low, as petitions presented to the House of Commons averred, that the workmen could not earn more than a halfpenny an hour. These indictments were certainly not comprehended by 33d Edw. I., (the statute of conspirators.) The words are, in the simple terms of those days,—" Conspirators are those

who bind themselves, by oath or otherwise, to indict,
or to move, or to falsely maintain pleas:" That is,
to do what these hosiers meant to do, bind themselves to indict the Lord Lieutenant, the mayor of
Leicester, &c., for protecting the poor people of
their county, in enabling them to earn a livelihood.
It is not a little singular that the modern legal authorities should construe the above 19 words to mean
that every man who should agree with another, to
restrain a third person, should be a conspirator,
within the meaning of the Statute, which certainly
only meant to restrain persons from maliciously
confederating together, to indict another person on
a false charge, or to sue him on false grounds. It
certainly only relates to confederacies to prosecute
suits at law.

The reign of George the Third, so remarkable
for great events, began, in some measure, very un-
propitious for servants, as by the Act 6th Geo. III.
cap. 25, servants and artificers were placed under
very heavy restrictions. By this Act, persons hiring
themselves for a term, and absenting or misbehaving
themselves, are liable to be imprisoned by one Justice, for not less than one, nor more than three,
months, and no appeal is allowed in cases of commitment. This, at first sight, may not appear objectionable or unreasonable, but it is the most cruel,
unjust, and oppressive statute in the code. By the
authority of this statute, any person who hires himself for a term, may, if he shall leave his work be-

fore the end of his term, notwithstanding any dispute
he may have with his master, or any unpleasant employment he may chuse to employ him upon, may
be imprisoned, and compelled to serve again. As
to misbehaviour, one Justice is to be the judge of
what may be so called; a few angry words, singing,
appearing dirty, smoking tobacco, workman not
finishing his work to please his master, or not doing
enough,—in short, every thing that the master
chuses to style misbehaviour, has been construed into
an offence before one Justice, who sends the unfortunate man to the gaol, or house of correction,
without an appeal; while the master, it has been
constantly held, can discharge such artificer or servant at a moment's notice, which has been frequently
done. These contracts have been made for 14
years, under the following specious pretences. A
workman is hired, by written contract, drawn up by
an attorney; the master tells the servant, " I shall
hire you at a certain ratio per week, but I do not
mean to give you those wages; I mean you to work
by the piece, at a price at which you will earn
double or treble the money. But then I cannot
promise you the price for ever; there is no knowing how trade may turn; I never mean to give you
the price in the contract, but I should not like to be
compelled to give more; you will have a regular
job of work. The contract, or bond, is all nothing,
but I have a secret in my factory which I don't wish
to have disclosed, and I am determined to have no

man in my employ who can leave me, and take my
invention to another master. This appears reasonable to the servant. They adjourn to the master's
attorney's office, who reads over the Agreement,
drawn up in law jargon, where all the hard words
in the language, and all the synonymous terms, are
huddled together; one half the words he never
heard before; the *saids* and *aforesaids* confound his
understanding, they might as well read Greek or
French to him. " You are to sign, (say they,)
are you agreeable?" " I suppose it's all right,"
says the workman to the master, " you know what
we had agreed on ; I cannot write my name, I will
put my mark to it. I should like a copy, (says the
workman,) to shew to a friend." " Why," says
Mr. Attorney, we never give copies ; but if your
master is agreeable, you shall have a copy for *half
a guinea*. " Are you any ways suspicious, that you
want a copy, John ?" says the master. " Oh, no,"
says John, " I know what we agreed upon." The
poor servant goes to work at the price agreed on,
upon piece work. At the end of a few months, his
master tells him that he shall reduce his price, or
shall make a deduction from his price for rent of
machine, or some other pretext. " That is not according to my agreement (says John) : I am determined to leave ; I'll work no more, unless you will
give me what we agreed upon." " I'll tell you what,
Jack, (says his master,) if you don't go to work
this instant I'll take you before a Justice, and send

you to the house of correction ; you shall dance upon the tread mill." " So I will go to work, if you will give me my price," says John. " We shall see," says the master. He applies to a magistrate for a warrant,—the man is apprehended before a Justice,—his friend the attorney attends, produces the Agreement, in which the workman agrees to work for half wages; " And here, (says the master, I have been giving him as much again. But as he has behaved himself so ill, I will now make him work to the *contract*. This pretty contract is read over by the Justice's clerk, and explained by the Magistrate to him. He now finds that he is obliged, under a heavy penalty, to keep his master's secrets, to work all night if his master chuses to employ him,—that his master can make him work to the letter of the contract. " Why, (says John,) I agreed to be paid by the piece, and that paper was to be all a sham, your Worship ; it was meant only to keep me from leaving him, which I don't want o do, if he will give me the *price agreed on*. "John, (says the Justice,) I have it here in black and white, that you agreed to work for so much per week, and you must go to work, or go to the house of correction." " Mayn't I have a copy of that paper, (says John,) for I'm sure all's not right, that's not my agreement." " Oh yes, you may and ought to have a copy," says the Justice. " Call at my office, (says the Attorney,) and you shall have a copy." John goes with half a guinea in his hand, (perhaps having pawned his Sunday coat,) obtains a copy,—his friends and him read it over, but, not being able to comprehend the jargon, another sage of the law is advised with, who, after charging him 3s. 6d. acquaints him that the Agreement is according to law, and he must go to work.

Many have submitted to the house of correction sooner than work. If a man is hired by a master for his own convenience, he ought to be bound to give the real wages agreed on, and ought also to be compelled to keep that servant the whole of the time for which the agreement was made, unless he can show sufficient cause to discharge him, before a Justice. No man ought to be sent to gaol, without an appeal, by one Justice, unless he is a well known and *convicted* rogue and vagabond. The master and servant ought to be reciprocally bound by their engagements. Some masters there are who never make any engagements with their workmen for wages, but pretend they do not know what others are giving,—that *when* the price is settled, and becomes general, then they will settle with their men. The men draw money upon account, and suppose that they have a large surplus to receive, when lo! if they are clamorous to be settled with, they are discharged, and make way for new dupes. The magistrates, in this case, have no power, as there is *no price agreed on.* Others *dock,* as they call it, 5 per Cent. for ready money, or deduct 25 per Cent. for alleged bad work, or will not pay any thing for the work, because they allege it is ill done. A very common practice has prevailed, of masters agreeing to give the usual or general rate of wages, and to deduct, as a bonus, from the workman, 25 per cent, and even 50 per cent, from the wages agreed on. This may perhaps excite some surprise, as to what can induce a master to make sham bargains for wages with servants. The reason is two-fold: first, to blind other masters in the same trade, by making it apparent that they give the same price as that usually given : and the other reason, that merchants and wholesale purchasers regulate the price which they give the master manufacturer, by the amount of the wages, materials, &c. If they reduced the wages openly, other masters would reduce their price also, and the merchant would require the goods at a lower price ; but if they can keep up appearances, they can pocket the wages. Some masters, by using threats to their work-people of being discharged, &c. have succeeded in keeping such transactions a secret for half a year or more together, and have pocketed such ill-got hundreds, until some new imposition has been attempted, a quarrel commences, and the matter is developed, to the great confusion of the manufacturing districts. In short, as to price agreed on, it is evaded in every possible way, and it is difficult for a great number of workmen to say, who are employed by these sharking fellows, what price they did agree on. There are so many ifs and ands, so much to deduct for this,—so much to be stopped for that,—so many demurs about work, and finishing, &c. &c. that in many manufacturing districts they catch what they can: if they were to talk about the price agreed on, to use their own expressions, they would " get the sack," that is, be turned away, nolens volens, without being told why or wherefore. Those persons who have not been conversant with manufacturing districts may perhaps think this account strange ; they imagine that a man must know, in some shape or other, what price he has agreed on for his labour; but there are hundreds of workmen in England who will prove that they have not known what they were to have for their labour until they got it, and this is a very general complaint in dull or flat trades, in the manufacturing districts. Is it any wonder that such work-people become wicked or dishonest, when such dreadful examples of overreaching and dishonesty are shewn them, by persons whom they regard as their superiors?

Though the code of restrictions, by preventing combinations of workmen, had been considerably augmented during the reign of George the Third, yet at the same time a very laudable and just spirit has prevailed, not to leave the servant or master without legal remedies in cases of disputes. In the year 1800, the same year, the general combination act was passed. An act was passed to settle disputes in the cotton weaving manufactures in England, and by a strange anomaly, nearly the very same words and provisions are contained in the 39 and 40 George III., cap. 106, general combination Act. One is the 39 and 40 George III., cap. 90, which relates only to cotton weaving, and Chap. 106, of the same year, makes the provisions of Chap. 90 extending to trades and manufactures in general, with the exception that the certiorari is taken away by the first and not by the second act.

The provisions for the settling of disputes are, that either master or journeyman may send to the other, a submission to arbitration, appointing and naming a person for his arbitrator, and requiring the other party to name an arbitrator within two days, to settle the dispute between them, who are empowered to summon witnesses and administer oaths; they are required to make their award in three days, which, if they neglect, either party may summons them before one justice, to state the points in difference between them, and the justice may either determine the difference or proceed to hear the witnesses himself *de novo ;* who is required to make his award within three days. The time may be extended by consent of both parties for making the award. Either party not performing the award when made by arbitrators or justice, to be imprisoned until he does fulfil it. Either party not submitting to arbitration, forfeit 10l. by distress and sale, or be committed not less than two nor more than three calendar months. In 1804, (44 George III.,

H

cap. 87) the cotton weavers' act was amended, and the power is taken from either party to send notice of arbitration, and requires the justice, on complaint made, to name not more than six nor less than four persons, one half of whom shall be masters or foremen, and the other half journeymen. The master to choose one master out of the masters or foremen nominated, and the journeymen one from the journeymen, who have full power to settle the dispute ; the justice to name the place of meeting, who are to determine the dispute in two days, exclusive of Sunday.

If any person making such complaint shall not attend such nomination to choose his arbitrator, proceedings to be quashed ; *or person not attending against whom complaint is made, the justice to choose one for him.* If an arbitrator being named shall refuse to act, the justice to name another. The arbitrators not agreeing, justice may decide. If upon nomination of a second arbitrator, *only one shall attend, he may hear the evidence and make the award.* Complaint in case of bad warp, &c. must be made in three weeks. Parties refusing to fulfil the award within forty-eight hours, forfeit 10l. by distress and sale of goods, or be committed for not less than two, nor more than three months.

Three very just and politic clauses were inserted in the 10th, 11th, and 12th Sections, which inflicts a penalty of not more than 40s. nor less than 20s. on the master or agent (if required by the workman) for not giving a ticket or note, stating the quantity of materials delivered out, the nature of the work to be performed, and the price agreed on for executing such work, against which the master has no appeal. The former acts did not include women or children, but by this they are expressly provided for, as the father, mother, husband, friend, &c. may sue.

The 17th Section fixes the justice's clerks and constable's fees. The fees are certainly very low, and may be contrasted thus with the fees charged in a large manufacturing town in the midland counties, and will shew the necessity of the enactment:

			charged by town clerk.		sometimes.	
	s.	d.	s.	d.	s.	d.
For each summons, allowed by this act,	0	6	3	0	6	0
For every oath, ...	0	6	1	0		
For drawing and entering order, ..	0	6	3	0		
For every warrant, ...	1	0	2	0	3	0
For every conviction, ...	1	0	4	6		
To constable, for service of summons,	0	6				
at same place			2	0		
— — — for executing warrant of distress and sale of goods ..	1	6				
at same place			5	0		
— — — custody of goods de- strained per diem	0	4				
— — — for every mile he shall travel	0	4*				

---

* To convict an offender, the fees of the clerk of the peace, and constable's charge, amounted to 2l. 1s. 6d., and in another

The year before, in 1803, by the 43 George III., cap. 151, these provisions had been enacted for Scotland, with this difference, that each party had the right of challenging twice peremptory, without shewing cause, and the master in case of the ticket is punished for not giving a ticket. In fact, the requiring is the way to have the act evaded, as an arbitrary rogue of a master would soon tell a workman, " Oh, you want a ticket, do ye? give me back my materials, I don't employ gemmen who want tickets."

This method of requiring masters to give out a ticket, when he delivers the material to be wrought up, is the best mode hitherto discovered for preventing frauds and disputes between masters and servants, and ought to be extended generally. Few masters would object to it; the greater number would think it an excellent regulation, and those that did object, would do it only on the ground of their own interest, as it would tend to prevent their petty peculations on their work-people. Surely no fair dealing man would object to enter in a workman's book the quantity of material delivered, the manner the work was to be made, and the price he was to have for making it; the man either is or ought to be told, he has now only his memory to trust to, in

---

case 1l. 19s. 6d.; costs of an order for payment of wages and constable, 19s. The constable charged 7s. for serving summons, 6s was charged for the summons, and the rest for drawing and filing the order for payment of wages.

the other case he might refer to his book, which would prevent mistakes and disputes. The master is almost necessitated to make the entries in his own book, and no sound reason can be given why a copy ought not to be given to his work-people ; as to the trouble, it would save trouble eventually, by causing business to be conducted in a regular manner, free from disputes and errors.

almost a contract

The provisions of the clauses respecting arbitrations, of 39 and 40 George III., cap. 106, have been found very inapplicable to settle disputes, as the lawyers have found means to evade it. The party who received notice of arbitration appoints an arbitrator, who refuses to act, saying he is perfectly satisfied. " I have heard," says he, " what my friend has to say ; I think that your party is wrong, besides, I have no time to attend just now." If asked when he can attend to hear the evidence, " Why, I don't know, call again to-morrow, I can perhaps give you an answer." In truth, he is appointed according to law, and he never means to arbitrate ; the party who appoints him, know, that they being the party who are required to arbitrate, are in the wrong, and consequently they use every effort to prevent the affair coming to a fair hearing. The party has then no resource but to apply to the justice, but then he must apply to the justice within the three days, and the justice can only take cognizance of the points in difference between the *arbitrators.*

Thus has this most excellent intentioned law been evaded, and has become nearly a dead letter upon the statute books. It has been found equally as equitable to the masters as their work-people, as when they leave them in debt, or in many other cases when they are likely to be defrauded by un-principled servants; this has been found a most ef-fectual remedy in disputes wherein the justices by law have no authority. As to the justices nomi-nating four or six arbitrators, who will undertake the arbitration, this must be difficult indeed, and must give the justice a great deal of trouble and unpleasantness. By the law, as it now stands, one person for each party is nominated to decide the dispute, who, if they disagree, may refer to the justice, but the law does not provide for an *umpire*, which would at once terminate the dispute without troubling the justice, who, perhaps, resides some miles from the place of dispute.

In 1817, the practice of paying workmen's wages in goods instead of money, had prevailed to a con-siderable extent in the steel, and steel mixed with iron, and plated and cutlery manufactures, and the 12 George I., cap. 34, was extended to those ma-nufactures by 57 George III., cap. 115, and by 57 George III. cap. 122, its provisions were ex-tended to colliers. The next year the 12 George I. was amended, and made applicable to the re-covery of the penalty; by the statute, the penalty, which is 10l., is directed one half to the informer and the other half to the party aggrieved ; now, as the workman who was paid in the goods necessarily was the principal witness, his testimony was objected to because he was an interested party, being entitled to a share of the penalty on conviction.

The courts of law having, since the reign of George I., decided that no interested person should be a competent witness, this statute became nugatory, as it became almost impossible to procure a third person present at these transactions. This had been obviated as to the woollen manufactures by 29 George II., cap. 33, which directs a penalty of 20l., one half to the informer and the other half to the poor. The 58 George III. went still further ; it provided, that in case the informer gave evidence, the penalty should all go to the poor. That is, where a workman made complaint and no informer appeared, the workman was made the informer and became a competent witness. This Act likewise provideth that where parties agreed to take bank notes they might be lawful payment for wages, the statutes requiring payment in good and lawful coin of the realm.

The last Act respecting masters and servants was 1 Geo. IV., cap. 93, which was an expiring law, enacted only for one year, and until the then next session of Parliament. This short lived statute enacted, that if any person who employed persons enumerated in former Acts, should either directly or indirectly make any restriction or agreement, or

cause such to be made, with any artificer, workman, or labourer, as to the manner of expending
his wages, or shall do any thing in violation of those
Acts, so far as respects the payment in wages, shall
forfeit and pay, *in lieu* of any penalties imposed by
the said Acts, the sum of not less than £10, nor
more than £20; the quibbling sages of the law,
who glory in reading across, declare that these
words do not inflict a penalty; they say that the
words should run,—*shall in lieu of any penalties*,
&c. forfeit and pay. This statute amended the
20th Geo. II., cap. 19, as to allowing masters
twenty-one days to consider whether they would
pay workmen or not, and directs the Justice to
name *his time*. In order to prevent appeals, the
Justices were empowered to order *treble* costs;
that is, if they pleased they might give *no costs* at
all ; (the *usual way*,) they were compelled to give
costs on conviction, but not on appeal. To frame
these Acts of Parliament, practical men ought to be
employed, who are aware of all the quirks, which
designing men take to evade the laws. There is
not the least doubt but the gentleman who drew up
this bill meant it to be effectual, and he thought it
would be construed according to the literal meaning,
but the gentlemen of the law construe Acts of Parliament almost to their own meaning, and unless some
check is put to the practice of construing words, &c.
an Act of parliament must be passed, enacting a
Dictionary, containing the lawful meaning of every

word in the English language. "You must construe
the statute strictly," say the lawyers, and immediately they begin to dissect the statute, word
by word; " Here, (say they,) is an omission: it
does not contemplate this or that offence; I hold
that the legislature never meant this;—or, if they
did, as the statute is to be construed strictly, I submit it does not comprehend the charge wherewith
my client is accused. This is addressed to a lawyer: the Recorder, or perhaps the Judge, is of the
same opinion, and an Act of Parliament is declared
to be useless; 'tis wrong worded, and has no
meaning. The Judge ought, or Recorder ought,
to petition the legislature to amend it, and suggest
what words ought to be used,—and not to let the
code of the laws, which he is appointed to enforce,
remain inapplicable and useless, until some Member
of Parliament discovers the error, and brings in a
bill to patch the code. This statute, (1st Geo. IV.,
cap. 93,) it was alleged, was suffered to expire,
on the ground that no law could be devised to prevent the practice of paying otherwise than in money,
but what could be and was evaded; and the bill in
progress through both Houses, met with some opposition, and was only allowed to pass for one year.
The ground of this opposition was, that masters and
servants, like all other persons, ought to be allowed
to make their own contracts; and that the law
ought not to interfere. This is a favourite doctrine
of *modern* political enconomists, who seem to think,

that provided a man agrees to any contract, he cannot be oppressed or injured. They do not, or will not, see the immense difference between masters and servants, and contracts for purchase in markets, contracts for renting land, houses, &c. In the market, a dealer has some hundreds of customers; persons who rent land or houses have some thousands of persons to deal with; but in manufactures, in many instances, there are not above a score masters, and they, from want of capital, or machines, or connexions, and various other causes, cannot employ, even if they were so inclined, each other's hands; in very numerous instances, the poor workman has Hobson's choice,—that master or none. To be sure it is a great consolation to him to be told, when instead of money he receives linen, cloth, or prints, who have been old shopkeepers, or old patterns, did not you agree to be paid in goods? what have you to complain of? did not you agree to be paid in goods? Such language the workmen regard as the most cruel of all mockeries; they have been taunted with it, and nothing can equal the rage wherewith they exclaim, "Why you know well I have not a move in the world; all the masters pay in goods, what am I to do? where am I to go? Talk of agreeing, (they exclaim,) it is not left to that; here I am goods or nothing."

'Tis very true, that no law was yet made, but what its provisions were either violated or evaded. There are persons in society whom no laws can make honest; mankind have been for thousands of years sedulously employed by severe punishments, even to destroying the individuals, to prevent thefts ; but the long lists of criminals shew that we are not more fortunate in our preventive system than our ancestors. The greatest discovery ever made to prevent thieving, was to destroy the necessity for thieving, by ameliorating the condition of the working classes, and thus take away the prime inducement, poverty.

The law inflicted a penalty of £20 for paying otherwise than in money. A master got, perhaps, £50 a week by the practice,—was convicted perhaps once of the offence in the quarter, paid £10, walked away a gainer of £500, laughing, and declaring that all such enactments were bad laws, and a restriction upon trade. The Justices, too, in the County to which this Act was particularly directed, refused to convict ; and what convictions were made, were somehow or other quashed for want of form.

Don't these gentlemen know, that by 28 Edw. III. they are liable to a fine of 1000 marks, and that by 4th Hen. VII., cap. 12, they are declared men out of credence, that is, their oaths are not to be believed in a court of justice.

But the grand pretext was, they evade the law. The master does pay the money,—the men know where the master's shop stands, and if they don't deal there they are discharged. Be it so ; they get the money, that is half the whole point gained. The shop will not obtain above one half the money given to the workman by the master. Let the man but have the money, he will deal with the shop to keep *appearances*, but as to taking the whole of his wages to the master's shop, some few may, but the majority, when they get the money, will never go and buy goods they don't want, to go a hawking when they have done, to please their master. They are not so fond of those kind of masters; some will be kept back for rent, for taxes, and under a hundred pretexts, and as to discharging, the master may discharge an individual, he will never discharge them by dozens, of which he will find offenders, should they ever finger the money. Compel the unprincipled masters to pay in money,—let the men but once touch it, and the shops will break up. This is now actually the case in that very County which this Act contemplated, where the men are paid in goods; they receive a ticket to go to the shop; they dare not trust them with the money. These are all barefaced pretexts: the real meaning of all this political economical jargon is,—reduce the rate of wages.

One step more in this " economy," and slavery is at hand immediately. If a man is to make any agreement, unprotected, which his master can impose upon him, he has only got to sell, or hire himself, for life, and then, by his own agreement, he may become the property of his master. Such has

been the want of employment in England, of late
years, that there have been a great number of persons
who would have sold themselves for life, to have had
victuals, lodging, and clothing. But such has been
the low value of the services of man, that few masters would have taken such persons, on those con-
ditions, without a large premium. So much for
" every thing finding its own level." As for the wisdom of the old French merchant's answer to Colbert, when he asked them what he could do to
encourage trade,—*Laissez faire,* " Let us alone,"
says he. But Colbert should have asked,—" Well,
but will you let your workmen alone? All rogues
hate laws: ask a thief what he thinks of the constables, the justices, and judges, and he falls into
the greatest invectives against them, and thinks,
and declares, that if one man is more ingenious and
daring than another, he ought to be allowed to
practise his ingenuity. Such is the case with every
man who wants to take an advantage of another;
he hates all restrictions which prevent him. Were
all men honest, what need of laws? and why suffer
masters alone to take dishonest advantages of the
very foundation of Society, the operative labourers?
and if this is suffered, depend upon it they will have
as little regard for the property of others, as the
masters have for their property, which is the produce
of their labour. We have the most industrious
population in the world : why does this happen?
because their wages have been hitherto the most

promptly paid of any nation. Pay a man in blan-
kets, in sack-bags, in prints, in linen, in potatoes,
&c. set him a hawking, and then get him to work
again if you can. As for the tread-mill curing him,
he will soon tell you, " I was paid in goods ; I began
hawking them ; I find there is plenty to be picked up
on the roads in summer time. I find I can live ; there
is always something in the fields to be got. I may
work a little, but I'll never work as I have done ;
besides, its no use ; one can get nothing but goods.
I don't mind working for a few goods, just to hawk
with, but never no more as I have done. I can live
better a gipseying ; and besides, I see more life."
Yes, yes, let the gentlemen go a hawking a bit, and
get them into the factories, mines, and looms again
if you can, from 12 to 16 hours per day, for from
5s. to 10s. per week, and that, too, paid in goods.
" What do I care for the tread-mill ?" says the
collier ; " it's not half such hard work as *holing*."
" As for working the mill," says the weaver, " I
had rather tread six hours than weave sixteen hours."
These kind of people soon learn the motto,—" No
catch me no have me ;" and set the laws at defiance. They soon learn the art which seems to
puzzle the political economist so much, namely, to
evade the laws.

At length a Bill has been submitted to the House,
to regulate masters and servants generally. It repeals all the Statutes which regulate masters and
servants, with the exception of those which relate to

apprentices; three Acts which relate to the payment of coal-heavers' wages in London; three Acts which give power to the magistrates of London and Middlesex to fix the rate of wages of silk-weavers, commonly called Spitalfields Acts; one for regulating colliers and miners in the working of mines; 39th and 40th Geo. III., cap. 77, and all the Statutes which relate to the breaking and destroying of machinery, &c. The whole number repealed is 37, and 7 are partly repealed, making 44 in the whole.

Clause 1, Repeals 33 Edw. I., and declares that masters, servants, or any other persons, shall not be indicted for a criminal conspiracy, for making any agreement or contract, respecting work or wages.

This clause is to prevent malicious prosecutions for conspiracy, if masters agree amongst each other not to give certain wages, or servants mutually agree not to take certain wages. By Statute, the law says the punishment shall not be more than three months' imprisonment; by a forced construction of 33d Edw. I., pretended to be founded on common law, persons have been imprisoned two years, and may be transported for 7 years.

Clause 2 and 3, Proposes to re-enact 12 Geo. I., 39 and 40 Geo. III.. sec. 1-17, to prevent masters or servants entering into bonds or agreements, to bind themselves not to give or take certain wages, work certain hours, &c. &c. by declaring them null and void. Any person being aggrieved by such contracts, may enter an action for damages, in the County where such agreement, &c. took place.

Could masters or their servants make such agreements or bonds legal, it would have the most oppressive effects, as masters would bind themselves in heavy penalties, when disputes with their workmen run high, not to give certain wages, &c., by which they might ruin themselves if such bonds were sought to be recovered. If journeymen were to make such bonds, they would certainly, in moments of irritation, imprison each other if they broke the bond. The Courts would be full of such suits, and they would have a direct tendency to fix the rate of wages in some instances ; where the masters entered into bonds, when the wages were low, they would remain low ; and when the workmen entered into them when wages were high, they would remain high; as nothing but the introduction of new masters and new journeymen could break such engagements, and bonds would be entered into by the journeymen, &c. not to learn such persons.

Clause 4, Declares all such bonds forfeited, and also wagers laid to bind themselves, the money to be forfeited.

The mere declaring bonds and contracts illegal would not prevent them laying wagers, depositing notes, &c. and the persons who held such wagers, being interested, would give up the stakes, if they were not liable to be sued.

Clause 5, Proposes that all masters hiring servants, in any manufacture, for any time less than one year, shall give such servant or workman a ticket or note, according to Form set forth, stating the period for which such servant is hired, the amount of wages to be given, what hours they are to work per day, and at what periods they are to be paid, whether by day, week, month, or more, and what description of work is to be done.

This clause is to prevent disputes, which frequently now occur, the agreements being generally *viva voce*. This clause is as much to protect an honest master from a dishonest servant, as to protect a servant from a dishonest master. The servant, if he is heard upon oath, as to the agreement for his wages, the magistrate is bound to take his testimony, unless the master can bring a third person to contradict him, which gives an undue advantage to the servant *over the master;* and, besides, it compels an agreemeut to be made before the work is begun, and would enable the Justice to decide at once.

Clause 6, Requires masters in any trade or manufactures, hiring workmen for more than one year, to deliver them a copy of such agreement for hiring, *gratis,* and directs it to be executed in the presence of one justice, and filed by the clerk of the peace; such deed, unless so executed, not to be binding.

This is to prevent sham contracts, or workmen being hired for years, without having the terms wherewith they agree fairly explained to them, and

I

that no illegal advantage may be taken, when the term of the engagement is to bind them to each other for a long term.

Clause 7, Proposeth, that no hiring shall be for a longer period than 5 years, unless in cases where the master has Letters Patent.

This is proposed to prevent indefinite engagements, as hirings for a long period do not allow a workman to improve his situation in life. Apprentices, though hired by indenture, and of tender ages, are limited to 7 years; surely their fathers ought to be limited to 5 years. In order to secure the master from any unfair injury, in keeping his business, masters holding Letters Patent, in which it may be necessary to keep their invention a secret, it is proposed to suffer them to compel their servants to remain with them during the term of the Patent.

Clause 8, Proposes to extend the provisions of the 43d Geo. III., cap. 151, and 44th Geo. III., cap. 87, to manufactures in general, by requiring the master to give to his servant a ticket, according to Form prescribed, of the quantity of material, the price he is to have for his work, number of tools delivered, what charges to be made for tools, or other charges.

This is proposed to prevent frauds on either side, and to compel masters to make an agreement with their workmen as to what price they are to have for their work, which, it is presumed, is but reasonable. It also provides, that in every case where fresh materials are delivered only, the quantity of materials only shall be entered,*unless there is an alteration in the price or nature of the work. As to trouble,which may be possibly urged, the entry is always made in the master's book, and he may have a few thousand *Forms printed* for a few shillings.

Clause 9.—Masters or work-people giving up, receiving, or destroying tickets, when given, liable to punishment.

The fair and honest masters, who form a very large majority, would give and pay by the ticket ; but those avaricious masters who are the bane of the manufactural districts, would give the ticket, according to law, and would then, to evade its enactments, require the ticket to be returned, either to themselves or an agent, or perhaps insist on the workman destroying it before their faces.

Clause 10, Proposes, no verbal or other agreement shall vitiate the ticket, and requires the master to give no more nor less than the sum specified in the ticket.

Without this proviso, the disputes would be endless. " I gave you the ticket," says the master. " Well, but (says the man) we had another agreement, in which you engaged to give me more, *and I will swear it.*" Or the master might say, " Since

---

* It may be objected, that in many cases materials are not regularly delivered ; in such case, where materials are not delivered, the price only need be stated, and the charges to be deducted.

I gave you the ticket you agreed for less,"—both which might be true, but how could a justice decide?

Clause 11.—No Servant or workman shall be discharged before the term of his hiring is expired, without his consent.

This is law now by 5 Eliz. cap. 4, and is nothing but just, that if a master requires a workman, for his interest, to give up his services to him for a certain time, though he may have many opportunities in the time to mend his situation, the master ought to keep such servant for the whole term, as it was to obtain permament employment that he was induced to engage.

Clause 12, Provides, that the master may make complaint to a justice of misbehaviour, &c., who may cancel the hiring; and gives the like remedy to the servant.

Clause 13, Declares what shall be considered misbehaviour in servants, and punishes them for such misbehaviour.

Clause 14. Workmen working by the piece, and not hired, may give 14 days' notice to the master that he intends to leave his employment, when he shall be at liberty so to do, whether he has finished his work or not. The master may summon such workman, before a justice, and if he can prove damage by such workman leaving his work unfinished, the justice may award damages, which, if the workman refuseth to pay, he may be committed.

This clause is to set the workman free from any tyrannical master, who may wish to detain him under the pretext of not finishing his work. There are a number of trades who are compelled, from the nature of their employment, to begin one article before they finish the other; and masters frequently, in some trades, deliver out as much work as will take a workman six months to finish. The compelling a poor workman to finish his work is worse than being indicted for conspiracy, or prosecuted for combination. Fourteen days is sufficient for a master to obtain another workman: he can stop the workman any day he pleases, and 14 days is sufficient notice in return; and if he can prove his damage, the justice may award it him: if the master cannot prove damages, of what can he complain?

Clause 15, Provides that masters shall not compel servants to work during the night without their consent.

Clause 16, Proposes to inflict a penalty on masters forcing their work-people to work at night. This has been practised in some districts, to the great detriment of the health of the workman, where men have been compelled to work from ten o'clock at night until 6 in the morning, during the dead of the night. None but those who have seen what ravages this practice makes in the health of the work-people can believe how cruelly this practice destroys the most robust constitutions. Being exposed to the air all night, is not, but in very few instances, pernicious to the health, if warmly clad ; but a workman in a warm factory having to go out into the cold night-air, it soon destroys him. He may consent to work at night, but why should he be compelled?

Clause 17, Declares payments for work or labour done, otherwise than in money or bank notes, null and void, and empowers the magistrates to levy the full amount of the wages agreed on, according to ticket, together with costs by distress and sale, but not to extend to household servants.

The discrepitancies of 12 Geo. I., cap. 34, and 29 Geo. II., cap. 33, have been endeavoured to be obviated; all the shuffles which may be adopted have been endeavoured to be provided against; not even excepting the ingenious shuffle which was provided against by 19 Geo. III., cap. 49, namely, not to employ, but to purchase the bobbin lace, and give goods in exchange; upon this vital subject, which is greater in its importance and ultimate effects than the bullion or paper questions, nothing can further be added, for want of room, than to ask every inquiring mind what he thinks will be the consequence, if the great mass of the artizans, handicrafts, husbandmen, and all other labourers, are paid in kind instead of money? and what effect it will have upon the national character, in placing those numerous classes at the disposal of the masters, (the most unprincipled is meant,) as to what

they shall eat, drink, or wear? As to the thing
finding its own level, it is notorious now, that with
a law on their sides, the workmen cannot keep their
ground, and that in most branches of manufacture
in the country, they are gradually losing their
power of resistance in making their bargains. What
will be the consequence, when there is no legal
bar? when a master may pay in cockle shells?
It is asserted, and believed, that there is a point in
reduction at which wages must stop: the enormous amount of poor rates, and the situation of
Ireland, completely falsifies the prediction, and the
idea of throwing trade entirely open, displays such
a field for consummate villany, that the mind of every
operative man sickens when he reflects upon what
he knows will be the inevitable consequences. It
is well known that there are persons in this life, of
such avaricious, ambitious dispositions, that they
would sacrifice any body of men, or any interests,
to accomplish their ends: it is this description of persons who regard all laws which impede their career
as the bars which will prevent them trampling on
society ; and there is no scheme they will not devise,
no tale they will not tell, *no hope* that they will not
hold out, *to those in power*, to be let loose, like hungry
tigers, to prey upon society. They know that misery
will take place, but what care they? " I know
it, (say they to themselves,) but I will always take
care to take the lead in every species of imposition.

I shall make a fortune ; what do I care, then, what becomes of the workmen, or the country ! I believe that all mankind would be villains if they knew how, and am I to blame if I can get the start of them?"

To prove that the masters generally detest the system of paying in goods, the master lace-manufacturers in the midland counties, subscribed nearly *one hundred guineas* to bring the late cause in the Court of King's Bench already mentioned, to a decision. Repeal all Acts which prevent masters paying in goods ; and collect taxes if you can, upon a population destitute of *real circulating medium* who will be paid in *shalligos and tickets. Ask the Americans what they think of their system of paying in goods, and they will not hesitate to tell you, it has broke up their factories. Clause 18, Proposes to re-enact 12 Geo. I., and 29 Geo. II., as to penalty for the first offence. And for the second, and every other offence, fine and imprisonment.

As to fine, the profits upon this practice are so great, in some large establishments, that £500 penalty would not prevent it; but then, it would be cruel indeed to visit a small manufacturer, who employs perhaps a man or two, with the same punishment: there remains no other alternative but personal considerations. Imprison the offender

---

* Shalligos is a cant term, used for checks of copper, or plated copper, made by masters, and paid their servants, which pass current the same as local bank notes, in limited districts, and at particular shops.

for his second offence, and there will be but few offenders.—The idea of fining a man worth 10,000l, and who gains £100 a week by the practice, in a 10l. penalty, is the greatest mockery upon the statute book. Touch him as you touch all other obstinate offenders against the laws, touch his person, and then see if you cannot prevent the system of paying otherwise than in money. But if you still proceed upon fines, " Oh, (says he,) when I am caught I'll send down my foreman, or my clerk, and I can get off for paying." But perhaps it may be asked, what, imprison a gentleman worth £10,000?—why not, if he acts against known laws, and is following an unjust practice, which is bringing misery upon his country, and sapping its greatness and prosperity? Why should not he feel the weight of the laws and justice of his country, as well as a poorer rogue?—Why should he be suffered to coin his linens or his damaged victuals into money,; and a fellow who makes a bad shilling be *hanged*, when the evil which is done to society bears no parallel in point of mischief?

Clause 19, Masters frequently lend money to servants, which it is not legal to stop again. This clause makes money advanced upon work to be done a legal payment, and empowers the master to make the stoppage. In many instances, masters have been deterred from lending money to servants, who were really honest people, because unprincipled persons have been found who have run in their debt, and then have refused, under one pretext or other, to allow them to stop their wages, which the magistrate was not authorised to allow.

Clause 20, Proposes to allow parents of children, or their guardians or friends, to sue for their wages. Great doubts have arisen on this point, as to whether the child must not sue in person; but least unprincipled persons should take advantage of this, it allows the child to sue in its own right. There are not wanting parents or kindred who would defraud such children; it allows children to summons in their own right, above 14 years of age.

Clause 21, Proposes to enable servants to recover wages from assignees, from the property only of the master. This is law now, by 43 Geo. III., cap. 11, and 44 Geo. III., cap. 87, in the cotton weaving manufactures.

Clause 22, Proposes to re-enact the 17 Geo. III., cap. 56, as to the punishing persons for embezzling materials delivered to them to work, by imprisonment only, and not by whipping.

As the law now stands, masters can only punish their servants who embezzle any hats, wool, linen, fustian, cotton, iron, leather, fur, hemp, flax, mohair, and silk manufactures, and clocks and watches, and the tools used in the above mentioned manufactures, except clocks and watches, also in the dyeing business, servants may be punished for embezzling materials, or dyeing without their master's consent; consequently, the greater part of the materials used, are unprotected when entrusted by a master to his servant to work up. Some of them, to shew the immense deficit of the law, will be enumerated:—hair, silk grass, skins, parchment, paper, wood, ivory, bone, horn, steel, brass, copper, tin, lead, pewter, zinc, gold, silver, platina, teutanic, glass, earths, stone, spar, marble, wax, paint, gums, fish-skin, and every other material as well as the tools or ingredients, if delivered to a workman to work up, can only be recovered legally by action of debt, or trover. It is certain that where materials have been taken without the consent of the master, from his premises, they have been indicted for the robbery; but where consent has been proved, and especially delivered to work up, the conviction has never taken place. This clause extends to all materials delivered to workmen, of whatever description, or denomination.

Clause 23, Proposes to alter the discrepitancies of 17 Geo. III., cap. 56, as to persons receiving embezzled materials, so as to render conviction more certain, and to alter the punishment for second offence to fine and imprisonment; and also to remedy the absurd enactment of being compelled, for second offence, to commit, or hold to bail to the Sessions before conviction.

Clause 24, Proposes to re-enact the 17th Geo. III., cap. 56, sec. 5, as to punishing persons who sell or deal in embezzled materials, knowing them to be unlawfully obtained,—a very extensive traffic in manufacturing districts.

Clause 25, Proposes to re-enact 17 Geo. III., cap. 56, sec. 6, to punish persons having materials in their possession, when they cannot account how they lawfully came by the same.

Clause 26, Proposes to re-enact and amend, so as to convict offenders who are found to have embezzled materials in their possession, or have deposited materials, which they cannot give an account how they lawfully came by the same, upon a Justice granting a search warrant, and punishing the person who deposited, instead of the person in whose house they may be found, if it shall appear that the householder was innocent of knowing them to be unlawfully obtained. This is a most desirable object, to break up those nests of vice, the receivers of embezzled or stolen materials, which cannot be effected as the law now stands, as explained before.

Clause 27, Proposes merely to re-enact the 17 George III., cap. 56, sec. 11, empowering constables, &c. to seize any person suspected of conveying embezzled materials in the night time.

Clause 28, Proposes, that in either of the two last cases the justice may grant time to produce evidence (on suspected persons entering into recognizance) as to how he became possessed of the materials.

Clause 29, Merely proposes to re-enact 17 Geo. III., cap. 56, sec. 13, that when any person shall be convicted of having such unlawfully obtained materials in his possession as aforesaid, they shall be placed in the hands of the churchwarden or overseer of the poor and advertised, and if the owner shall appear, to be returned to him on paying the costs, &c. ; if no owner appears, to be sold, one half the value to be given to the informer the other to the poor.

Clause 30, Proposes to re-enact 17 George III., cap. 56, sec. 17, as to journeymen dyers dyeing, &c. without consent of their employers.

Clause 31, Proposes to enable masters to recover their tools, &c. upon giving 14 days' notice, but not before materials are finished without consent of the workman. This extends to tools of any manufacture.

Clause 32, Extends the provisions of clause 31, to tools let out to hire, but not to enable persons to recover tools before the period for which they are hired is expired.

Clause 33, Proposes to enable justices to seize such tools by warrant, if not delivered up, and restore them to the owner.

Clause 34, Proposes to empower justices in case materials are damaged or lost, or destroyed either by accident or otherwise, to order the workman to pay for them, either by instalment or otherwise ; in default of payment, as directed, to be committed. If the master now receives any such money as compensation, it becomes a debt, and masters not unfrequent ly lose their property from unprincipled servants, imposing upon generous masters who are unwilling to prosecute for the embezzlement, unless upon sure grounds ; they have now no alternative but to pro-prosecute or receive by instalments, by which they are frequently seriously defrauded.

Clause 35, Proposes to enable the workman, upon giving up such tools, to summon the owner of such tools before one justice, who is empowered, if he shall think fit, to award him a recompence for his apparatus, if he shall have applied any such appa-ratus, or shall have lost any time, or been at any expense in preparing, repairing, or putting such machine to work, to be recovered by distress and sale. Nothing can equal the loss which journey-men sometimes sustain on this account, which has already been treated of.

Clause 36, Proposes, that if workmen wilfully neglect or injure tools, the master may summon them before a magistrate, who may cause them to pay such sum of money as he shall think fit, by in-stalments or otherwise, which, if he neglects to per-form, to be committed. It is doubtful which are the greater sufferers, the master or the workmen, in these cases. The workmen frequently so far neglect their tools when unemployed, as to become nearly useless lumber, and frequently pull them to pieces to apply to various other purposes, for which the master has now no remedy, only in case of taking parts away ;—if they are broken, rendered useless by rust, dirt, &c., the master has now no remedy against a careless worthless servant, who not unfrequently laughs the master to scorn when he sees the destruction of his property.

Clause 37, Proposes, that workmen, &c. taking tools or materials not actually delivered to them to work, shall, if they exceed the value of 40s., be guilty of felony.

This is a most crying grievance on both masters and men, as when materials or tools are missing in a factory the whole of the men are suspected.

Clause 38.—Receivers of such tools, &c. knowing them to be so obtained, to be guilty of felony.

Clause 39, Proposes to allow masters to inspect their materials in the day-time, and punishes workmen for refusing to suffer them to examine their tools and materials. Provided, that if it shall appear to the justice that the workman had applied any new invention, &c., then, upon proof being made on oath, that such materials, &c. are forthcoming in a proper state of preparation, such justice may dismiss the complaint.

This proviso is absolutely necessary to protect an ingenious workman in his secret of working. Why should the master be allowed to inspect his secret, which is the journeyman's property, the fruits of his genius and study, provided proof is made that his materials and tools are forthcoming, and in a proper state of preparation?

Clause 40, Proposes to amend the 39 and 40

George III., cap. 106, sec. 18, and empowers either masters or servants in any trade or manufacture, in all cases of dispute or difference, to nominate an arbitrator on their respective behalf, and requires the other party to name an arbitrator, by delivering copies of such submission to arbitration to the other party, and empowers the arbitrators to hear and determine the cause, and make an award, to be binding and conclusive to both parties.

Clause 41, Proposes, that the party who is required to name an arbitrator shall fix the time and place of meeting, by returning one of the copies received, appointing such place of meeting, which, if he shall neglect, the other party may name such time and place of meeting. It has been the practice to refuse to name a place of meeting.

Clause 42, Proposes to empower either the parties, or the arbitrators, to appoint an umpire or third person to decide with the arbitrators. This is not now legal, and an umpire, if appointed, would have no power.

Clause 43, Proposes, that when either of the arbitrators neglect to attend, either party may apply to a justice to name a place of meeting, by giving notice to the parties and arbitrators of the time and place appointed, when, if only one arbitrator attends, he may proceed alone.

This allows of no shuffling, and goes to decide the question at once. The party who does not provide an arbitrator to attend, is, it is presumed, in the wrong, and seeks to evade an equitable adjustment.

Clause 44, Proposes to empower either of the arbitrators to summon witnesses according to form, who, if they shall neglect or refuse to attend, may be brought before a justice and committed; this is by 39 and 40 George III., cap. 106.

Clause 45, Proposes, that where arbitrators cannot agree as to choice of umpire, or make their award, the justice may make the award.

Clause 46, Proposes, that the justice may appoint an umpire to decide the dispute on his behalf. The disputes frequently relate to technical matters, which the justice of the peace has little or no knowledge of, but yet, by the existing law, he is required to decide, which have frequently placed justices of the peace under very embarrassing circumstances, and has been one reason why an arbitrator *would not decide;* but if he was allowed to appoint a competent and skilful person on his behalf, he would be relieved from a great deal of toil, and having to appear before a competent person would soon and equitably be decided. One great reason why this wise and beneficial act has been rendered of little comparative use, is because the justices in many instances found themselves unavoidably incompetent to decide technical disputes.

Clause 47.—That in case a justice shall nominate an umpire, each party may have one challenge;

K

that is, provided the justice should nominate an improper or prejudiced person, which such justice may very innocently do, not to leave them without remedy.

Clause 48, Proposes, that in order that arbitrations may be cheap and summary, that no barrister, attorney, &c. shall be appointed as an arbitrator or umpire; were professional men to be chosen, the expense would be great, and the learned or professional man would undoubtedly puzzle the other arbitrator, and consequently protract an amicable adjustment.

Clause 49, Proposes to empower parties to extend the time for making the award, but should one party prove obstinate, the justice, if he shall think fit, may extend the time.

Clause 50, Proposes to re-enact 39 and 40 Geo. III., cap. 106, as to inflicting a penalty of 10l. on persons refusing to arbitrate, or the whole amount of the matter in dispute. It has not unfrequently happened, that the matter in dispute has been more than 10l., in which case the other party would sooner pay the penalty than arbitrate.

Clause 51, Proposes, that if either party shall refuse to fulfil the award, he may be committed for a definite time. As the law now stands he is to be committed until he shall fulfil the award, which may be for years.

Clause 52, Proposes, that masters may depute agents to act on their behalf.

Clause 53, Proposes, that persons receiving materials under false pretences, shall be punished the same as receiving embezzled materials.

Clause 54.—Justices may make allowances to workmen for waste ; hitherto the master could demand the whole of his material without the magistrate having power to allow for waste.

Clause 55, Proposes to fine masters for delivering short weight, or using any fraudulent means by damp or otherwise, to increase the weight, &c. This has been a great grievance to many an honest workman, who ought to be protected from fraud.

Clause 56, Proposes to commit work-people for using any fraudulent means to increase the weight or quantity of their materials to defraud the master, provided that the workman shall not be punished for using ingredients, &c. to prepare his materials for working, provided they are in general practice. The practice of using grease, soap, allum, clay, &c. &c. is a most intolerable grievance to masters, by which they lose great quantities of materials, and hundreds of dishonest persons obtain a livelihood by vending them.

Clause 57, Proposes to re-enact the 43 George III., cap. 151, as to workmen in the cotton weaving manufacture in Scotland, working by the standard ell.

Clause 58, Gives power to the justices to summon witnesses. It is not a little singular that justices of the peace out of sessions have not a general power to compel the attendance of witnesses.

Clause 59, Proposes to empower the justices to administer oaths.

Clause 60.—Justices being masters in the particular trade, incompetent to act.

Clause 61, Proposes, that justices refusing to act may be sued. It is no uncommon thing for justices of the peace to refuse to act, stating that the law in various cases is a bad law, that they don't think it proper to interfere, and a number of other lame excuses, which they not unfrequently make either from humour or partiality. As to obtaining writs of mandamus, the expense is great, and two or three terms may intervene before the writ can be obtained, and then the justice condescends to begin when the affair is all gone and past, and the party complaining has spent 50 or 60l. By the statute of 43 George III., cap. 141, justices of the peace being sued, unless *malice* is proved, can only pay two-pence damages. Many other things can be proved which are improper besides malice. Thus a justice of peace giving instructions to an offender, how, in his opinion, to evade the law, from partiality, and because he was addicted to the same offence, is improper; the old laws are very severe on justices of the peace refusing to put the laws in execution.

Clause 62, Limits the time for bringing actions against magistrates.

Clause 63.—Inhabitants of a parish good evidence; that is, objections have been taken by the lawyers where part of a penalty goes to the poor of the parish, that every inhabitant was an interested person, incompetent to give evidence. Oh, disinterested men!

Clause 64, Proposeth, that where it shall be necessary to call a party aggrieved as evidence, his being entitled to a remuneration (if the justice shall think fit) shall not be construed to vitiate his testimony as an interested person.

Clause 65, Proposes to compel offenders as well as other persons to give evidence, and indemnifies them from the consequences of being prosecuted.

As the law now stands, if a workman is called upon to give evidence to whom he has sold his materials, instances have occurred of informations being laid against him for selling embezzled materials upon his own statement.

Clause 66, Proposes, that proceedings shall not be quashed for want of form, and allows the justice, if objections are taken, to amend the conviction or order.

Most of the acts of parliament state, that proceedings shall not be quashed for want of form, and yet they are quashed for want of form, which the lawyers always declare are for want of substance. A conviction stated, a person convicted should be imprisoned two months, the act said not less than three months; the conviction was quashed, and before a new warrant could be issued the offender absconded. Nothing is so common as for clerks of the peace to make errors in the convictions; there is no law to punish them for doing so, though there is strong suspicion that it is done purposely. They have even made errors as to the county in which the fact was committed, and convictions have been quashed on that account; nay, even the warrant for the order of the payment of wages was quashed in the Court of King's Bench, on the 30th April last, on the express ground that it had not followed the form of the act, though the 17 George III., cap. 56, sec. 22, declares that proceedings shall not be quashed for want of form. A lawyer, if he has got a bad cause, always takes an objection to the conviction, and offenders upon this weak ground often escape. A justice of the peace, or his clerk, though obliged for decency's sake to convict, often contrive that the conviction shall be wrong, because they have a partial bearing to the party, or because *they think* the law is too severe, or wrong in its principle, and thus defeat the ends of justice. The prosecutor has no remedy, he has paid fees, feed attorney and counsel, brought up his witnesses, and then he is told there is an error in the *conviction*. " You can begin again," says the court, " if you please." " Yes," says one bluff fellow, " but will you find me the money?" It may be all very well for the lawyers, but it obstructs justice. " What would even a savage say, if he was told there was an error in the conviction? He would answer, " Then mend it : is the man guilty ?" " Yes." " Then why let him escape ?" What is the answer that must be given ?—" Oh no, that cannot be, the lawyers would lose their fees! better one half the rogues in the country escape than for the lawyers to lose their fees."

Clause 67, Proposeth, that persons convicted shall have a copy of their conviction, and all orders, determinations, or dismissals of cases, the Justice is required to give a copy thereof. As to copies of convictions, a copy is generally refused, until the night before the Sessions ; and many Justices dismiss cases in the loosest manner imaginable, without assigning any motive, or scarcely give the parties an opportunity to state their case.

Clause 68, Directs how penalties are to be applied.

Clause 69, Proposeth to allow an appeal to both the accuser and the accused. As the law now stands, none but the accused can have an appeal ; and complaints have been frequently dismissed, by single Justices which would certainly have been convicted at the Sessions. Nothing is so common in the country as for the Justice to be spoke to ; that is, some friend, either of the defendant or plaintiff, who is an acquaintance of the Justices, goes to him, and very kindly acquaints him of the *whole* merits of the question, the motives of the opposite party, the good character of his party, and many other representations, *all generally very true.* The Justice, by this means, is made wiser than either the accuser or the accused; he is put in possession of the *secret,* and he acts accordingly: that is, according to the wishes of *his friend.* He comes prejudiced to the decision; he has been told *the character* of the opposite party, and he has made up his mind what to do when the case comes before him. Many of the best intentioned men have been thus imposed upon, and it has become quite a system, to get somebody, in most cases of prosecution, *to speak to the Justice.* But if the Justice supposed that these cases would come before the public, he would think twice, investigate, and the whole plot would be developed, and the vile system of speaking to the Justice, would, in a great measure, be abandoned. There are a great number of Justices, who would ring the bell for their servant to shew such persons to the door, who came to bias them; but there are many more who, from curiosity, (though well intentioned men,) would listen, and, God knows, we are all weak enough to be imposed on by first impressions.

Clause 70, Provides, that no appeals shall be made in any order, or conviction, or matter connected therewith, for any sum under 30s.

Clause 71, Proposes to prevent proceedings being removed by certiorari. This requires no comment, as all laws which respects servants, if they can be removed by certiorari, the law does not apply to them, 'tis utterly impossible for them to pay the expense of such legislations.*

Clause 72, Provides that this bill shall not extend to Ireland.

Ireland has but lately been united in legislation with Great Britain, and the laws which ought to regulate Ireland ought to undergo a separate consideration, from the difference of manners, circumstances, customs, and feelings of the people of Ireland. The Irish Statute Book requires to be calmly and attentively examined, to keep what is good, and reject what is obsolete and bad; and, what is still more essential, to inquire into what is the effect of those laws, by an actual inquiry among the servants and masters in Ireland. Nothing is so easy as to make enactments, but nothing is more difficult than to make good and proper laws, which are applicable to the persons and their circumstances for whom such laws are intended. What may be a good law in England and Scotland, may be oppressive in Ireland, either

---

* The 20th Geo. II., cap. 19, takes away the certiorari, but then only 5l. can be recovered. The foregoing remarks respecting the certiorari were inserted by mistake, too late for correction : they apply to 22 Geo. II., cap. 27. In manufactures where artizans are employed, the middle man, or undertaker, frequently takes work to employ twenty men; and if he can recover only 5l. what remedy has he ? Besides, it is not unusual for servants, in manufactures, to come to a settling once in a month, or even in six months.

upon the master or the servant'; which every legislator ought carefully to avoid.

It may be asked, does this bill contain all the law necessary to govern masters and their servants? The answer is, No, it does not relate to apprentices; the apprentice laws are in strange confusion, for they have, if possible, been more patched than the laws respecting masters and journeymen, &c. To make just, equitable, and applicable laws, for the government of apprentices, is a very difficult matter, and requires considerable technical knowledge. To frame a code for the education of the youth who are to be operative artizans of this country, requires the greatest care and attention, for one bad law may ruin thousands of young men; and as the practice of apprenticing youth is so much altered from that of our forefathers, great care ought to be taken to make the law applicable to those new relations, namely, out-door apprentices, which are more in the nature of hirings than what was formerly conceived to be apprenticeship. Something, however, ought to be done in this respect, for the youth of England are in a most deplorable state.

This Bill provides for settling disputes upon a small scale, between individuals; but disputes upon a large scale are totally omitted. How far it would be prudent to legislate, when disputes are upon a large scale, is a matter of grave and weighty consideration. Our forefathers would allow of no disputes; *they settled at once what was to be done.*

We now seem stark mad on the other extreme, and every man is now to dispute or not, and fight his own way in the world. In plain terms, each of you do the best for yourselves : down with all re-strictions or regulations,—a scramble for ever!!! To use the homely language of the vulgar,—the best dog will leap the stile. But has it occurred to those enlightened personages, who can see all the faults of their forefathers by the light which shines so bright in the 19th century, what rogues this pretty system of theirs is making in old England? Do they think that when they have set every man's hand against his fellow, to make the best bargain he can, and, if possible, overreach his neighbour,—that they can make him honest again? Do they think they shall be able to manage a nation of rogues with the same facility as when they were honest men, and had a respect for each others' rights? Ask your neighbouring nations,—Do you think that when you have taught your population every one to take care of themselves, that your gene-rals will be enabled to say, " I made mistakes which would have ruined the generals of any other coun-try ; but my troops held together, and fought me out of the scrape?" Yes, yes, the Lancashire man is taught to be " jannok," the Londoner to be " stout," but if ever the day comes which this sys-tem of legislation proposeth, *the enlightened system of the* 19*th century,* every man will, when in dan-ger, take *care of himself,* and you will hear in your ranks, spite of the drummer in the rear, the dreadful cry of the French,—" *Sauve qui peut!*" and, "the devil take the hindmost." Recollect, legislators, that these new doctrines are those from France,— from the enlightened club of *economists* of PARIS. Do you think if the English troops had been in the same situation at the battle of Waterloo as the French, that they would not have effected a retreat? Do you think that they would have become a mob, because they were overpowered? No, no, you know better. But make them selfish,—destroy every restriction, set them one upon another, and then see the result : the rising generation will be a far different race of men from their fathers, owing to this system having begun its operations amongst us.

Having gone through the whole of the laws applicable to masters and servants, which have been passed at different periods, from the earliest times down to the present day ; and shewing, as far as the limits of such an undertaking would allow, the motives which apparently prompted the legislature at different times to adopt them, and having, it is presumed, fairly shewn their inapplicability to the present relative situation of masters and servants, and having also given a brief outline of the proposed Bill, and the reasons for each enactment, it only remains for us to explain what has induced us to accompany such a Bill with any remarks at all. In the first place, it must be recollected it is the only attempt since the days of Elizabeth, that has been made, to frame a code of laws for the general regulation of master and man, which, even had it rested on its own merits, would have been sufficient to call for some explanation of the grounds upon which it was founded. Considering, therefore, that in order to make some room for its due efficacy, it is necessary to pull down the old fabric, and erect a new one upon its original, ancient, and scattered ruins, which, it will be allowed, is no light undertaking, let it be attempted by whomsoever it may, the following remarks have been thrown out, though perhaps somewhat warmly and pointedly expressed, for the consideration of those who may think it worth their while to pay any attention to what we consider, (whether justly so or not,) a subject of the utmost importance.

In conclusion, we have only to add, that in the foregoing Remarks, neither masters nor servants, nor lawyers nor legislators, are intended to be attacked or calumniated as a body ; our object is only to *attack the vices*, and *remedy the errors*, which every candid mind will allow have, from time to time, (as they ever will,) crept in amongst mankind, from the natural infirmities of our nature.

Our object was not to attack any man, or body of men, but to attack *principles* which we conceived to be wrong in governing society, and instead of being, (as is too much the custom of the present day,) mere grumblers, have, as far as our humble abilities would enable us, endeavoured to point out remedies.

We therefore submit ourselves and our thoughts to the criticisms of others, as fearlessly as we have exercised our own, hoping that the same good temper and feeling which we trust have guided us, will actuate those who may not think exactly as we do. And, to use the language of an eminent statesman* of the present day, beg they will recollect, " We are all embarked on board the same boat, (*our country*,) and must sink or swim together."

---

* Mr. Huskisson.

FINIS.

G. SIDNEY, Printer,
Northumberland-street, Strand.

British Labour Struggles:
Contemporary Pamphlets 1727-1850

An Arno Press/New York Times Collection